WSB&G

A San Francisco Memoir

Judy Berkley

WSB&G
A San Francisco Memoir

ISBN: 979-8-218-04319-3

San Francisco in the 1980s
Legendary saloon, Washington Square Bar & Grill

Dedicated to the memory of
Sam Deitsch
With gratitude and great affection

ON THE MENU

1

Will the Stars Align?

One afternoon in 1977, I stood outside the double doors of Washington Square Bar & Grill and contemplated the scene. A couple trees sprouted from cuts in the concrete and softened the lines of the sidewalk. Awnings shaded a row of windows that gave an oblique view of Washington Square Park. The second story had a series of bay windows for activities having nothing to do with the business.

The architectural arrangement was typical of North Beach where Italian delicatessens, bakeries, bars, restaurants, and shops were at street level, surmounted by extra space and living quarters in wooden structures from previous decades. The intersection of commerce with community on every street gave North Beach the flavor of a real neighborhood, one that was holding the line against encroachments from Chinatown and the hustling Financial District.

That afternoon, I was job hunting, a task I disliked so much that I rewarded myself with a glass of wine for each restaurant I approached. I had been to three. Thus, I was, uh, relaxed when I entered WSB&G and came face-to-face with the saloon's co-owner, Sam Deitsch. His appearance was unlike anyone I'd ever seen. He had a little boy body, heavily freckled pale skin, a sparse beard, a head of scruffy hair, and he peered through over-sized spectacles.

Wavy Gravy aka Hugh Romney of the Merry Pranksters said "A sense of humor is a good survival tool." Given his odd appearance and diminutive size, I imagined Sam needed a Swiss Army knife.

Sam was dressed in tennis shoes, blue jeans, button-down oxford shirt, with a twisted red bandana knotted around his neck. He wore the same thing every day except when he added a navy-blue blazer for formal occasions. Despite his odd appearance and eccentric wardrobe choices, Sam projected self-assurance with cordiality. I liked him immediately.

What Sam saw was a 31-year-old woman, who already had many adventures in many places, nevertheless internalized a sense of Not Enough. Not slim enough. Not attractive enough. Not smart enough. However, I was Funny Enough. Perhaps, too much. Stuff popped out of my mouth that made people laugh. And, often made me cringe afterwards. Sam picked up on the funny stuff. He invited me to have a couple drinks with him at the bar and jokes and stories were soon flying.

On the surface, Sam's life seemed privileged. He was born in New York City to a well-to-do family of Jewish clothiers. He attended a private school for boys but chose to pursue the "higher education" of bartending in the vibrant saloon scene of Greenwich Village.

Sam's sister, Frances, who was two years older, went to Temple University, then, seeming to follow in the family footprints, studied at the Fashion Institute of Technology in New York City. But, Fran's career path made an abrupt lane change when she met Jay Landesman, whose clever, enterprising clan was based in St. Louis, Missouri.

When "Fran" married Jay, the couple relocated from New York to Gaslight Square in St. Louis and began building an entertainment mecca at the Crystal Palace nightclub. Eventually, Sam followed and invested in the nearby Golden Eagle Bar. The list is long of nascent talent that went through that Landesman/Deitsch nexus and on to major stardom. Sam seemed to know absolutely everybody in the entertainment world.

For all that wealth and glamour and rubbing elbows with celebrities and his plucky self-confidence, I came to feel Sam was sad at his core. He never married and his dating life was a private matter. Fran, who became a famous lyricist and poet, wrote a song thought to be inspired by Sam, "Ballad of the Sad Young Men."

Sing a song of sad young men, glasses full of rye
All the news is bad again, kiss your dreams goodbye
All the sad young men, sitting in the bars
Knowing neon lights, and missing all the stars.

Those melancholy sentiments were echoed in Sam's bittersweet words of comfort to his lovelorn female friends. He'd put a brotherly arm around their shoulders and say "There, there, nothing will be okay."

Laughter (and alcohol) were salves for a lonely heart. Sam relished the company of clever people and hired staff, which could enhance an environment that was always crackling with intelligent *bonhomie.* Being overqualified for the job was a qualification. Adding humor was a plus. Our mutual quest to extract laughter from life was a basis for friendship that sweetened the boss/employee relationship.

In due course, Sam and I had a ready source of laughs from the British humor magazine, *Punch.* For years, a lovely couple I met in London, subscribed to *Punch* in my name, during the editorship of Alan Coren. He was a composite of education at Oxford, Yale, and UC Berkeley, so his hilarious takes on contemporary foolishness appealed to me as an American Anglophile.

A habitual skeptic, Sam needed convincing that Coren was up to his humor standards. We were both acquainted with great humor writers and fierce wits; Benchley, Twain, Thurber, Dorothy Parker, SJ Perelman, Woollcott, Waugh, Wodehouse et al. So, he was dubious when I lauded Alan Coren. After reading a few examples, Sam demanded I pass along each and every copy to him.

> *A humorist tells himself every morning, "I hope it's going to be a rough day." When things are going well, it's much harder to make the right jokes. —Alan Coren*

Sam's ability to crack me up was almost on par with Alan Coren. His irreverent, sometimes abrasive wit, was utterly unregulated. A friend of his stopped in for a drink and asked me to convey his presence to Sam. A few minutes later, Sam asked where his friend was. I replied he'd had a quick drink and left. Sam shrugged his shoulders and said "In and out—like a minister's dick."

A raffish comment from Sam was a rarity. Around women, he was always a gentleman, which in the 1980s was a welcome respite from sexual come ons. Certainly, he was open to *more*, but his female friends could feel safe from pressure when in his company.

On that day in 1977, having drinks at the bar, Sam said a position might be opening up, but they would be looking for "…[A] star, a star of the bar."

I wrote my phone number on a cocktail napkin and brazenly added a star. Inside I thought, "Me, a star? Nope. Not Enough."

Ed Moose was on vacation when Sam hired me. I'd been working for about two weeks before meeting WSB&G's other partner. Ed was an imposing presence. He was well over six feet tall, swathed in XL tweeds, sported distinctive ties and suspenders, and had an itchy energy that was disconcerting. His handsome face struck me as a smudged image of William F. Buckley, Jr., a likeness Ed, a diehard Democrat, must have deplored.

Apparently, Ed didn't think a cocktail napkin job application was adequate. He grilled me in a way that suggested I was about to be un-hired. The crux of his examination seemed to be "Who do you know?"

Fortunately, I could give him the name of Bob Gattis, the manager at The Refectory in Dublin where I tended bar, and a lawyer I dated, who was something or other with East Bay MUD, the utilities district. That slim resume satisfied Ed for the moment and he could move on to being indifferent and, eventually, annoyed, with me.

The contrast between the two partners and their vastly different styles became clear from the start. When I was still getting acquainted with my new job, a couple came in after the lunch rush and took a window seat. The man was antagonistic from the get go. From years of experience, I was aware that some people, for reasons I'll never understand, want to spoil the pleasant pastime of eating and drinking with foul temper. And, doing so in front of a date was even more baffling.

The twosome was going to share a bottle of red wine. When I brought the glasses and presented the bottle, a California red, not a Chateau Margaux, the man was enraged that, somehow, I wasn't deferential enough to the wine. "Don't treat it cheap!" he yelled. Startled by the attack, I excused myself, went to Sam, and explained a customer had a complaint about my service. From his table, Sam peered across the room at the complainant, who, unbeknownst to me, was a writer with a world-wide reputation on the subject of tea and related customs. "That's Norwood Pratt," said Sam "Aptly named Pratt."

Sam went to Pratt's table, told him to get out, and never come back. In bar parlance, Pratt had been 86ed. Harrowing the clientele of grumpy jerks to create a convivial meeting place was part of the process that built WSB&G and was largely Sam's province. He told me "Taking crap is not part of your job."

Ed had a much higher tolerance for jerks, especially those with some claim to fame. While he would institute rules to reduce taking crap that affected how the business was run, he would easily contradict his own dictates. At one staff meeting, he laid down the law about *zabaione*. The warm, frothy, Italian concoction required one of the two cooks to step back from the hectic task of getting out the regular orders to whisk together egg yolks, sugar, and Marsala wine, in a copper bowl over a boiling water bath. Ed said, it was simply too disruptive to the flow of food preparation, especially during lunch, so no one was to take an order for zabaione. Got that, staff? No one!

Shortly thereafter, during a particularly frantic lunch, I was waiting on writer, poet Richard Brautigan. The peak of his popularity, surrounding his novels *Trout Fishing in America* and *Watermelon Sugar,* had passed. But, he was very popular in Japan, which was mystifying that a society known for courtesy and exquisite ceremonies, lionized a person as rude as Brautigan.

His lunch companions were two Japanese women, who, despite language differences, seemed to sense something amiss in his ill-mannered conduct. When they had finished their entrees, Brautigan announced imperiously they would have zabaione for three. I replied that zabaione was not available. Brautigan pitched a fit and demanded to speak to Ed, who approached the table rubbing his hands together as he typically did in the presence of celebrities.

"Of course, you can have zabaione, Richard. Judy will be happy to take your order," said Ed unctuously. For good measure, he shot me an accusatory look as though I had initiated the problem. That was an early skirmish of Deflection Dodge Ball, which is practiced by bosses, who cannot be wrong, but must lob blame at someone.

In 1984, Brautigan shot himself in the head with a .44 Magnum, ending a life of chronic alcoholism and, reportedly, abusive relationships. Sam, who was incapable of fake emotions, noted Brautigan's snail trail of incivility through the neighborhood, when he said "Today, there are bartenders all over North Beach drinking a toast."

Sam and Ed: How did two such different men with such different styles create the most popular restaurant and saloon in San Francisco history and raise it to national prominence? The story began back at Gaslight Square. Ed Moose was a native of St. Louis where he grew up Irish and Catholic, in a family that had financial setbacks. Nevertheless, he assembled an impressive, mishmash resume: He earned two degrees at St. Louis University. Passed through a seminary. Ushered at Cardinal baseball games (where it seems, he was bit by a baseball bug.) Served in an Army Special Forces unit. Utilized a degree in psychiatric social work to counsel disturbed children and distressed married couples. Fundraised for good causes. And, at various points, did some newspapering. Ed invariably described his employment history, prior to becoming a bar owner as "do-gooder jobs."

While working as the alumni director of St. Louis University, Ed was drawn to the jazz scene and conviviality of Gaslight Square, and the copious cocktails Sam poured at the Golden Eagle. He and Sam formed a lasting friendship that included a charming woman with a chandelier-shattering laugh, Mary Etta Presti, who became Mrs. Moose. The three of them relocated to San Francisco and occupied a two-flat home on Telegraph Hill. In the decade I worked for them, I never saw disagreement or disrespect. They seemed to share a genuine, enduring bond that weathered all storms.

For a time, after relocating to San Francisco, the threesome was at loose ends. Ed and Mary Etta worked various jobs, until Sam, perambulating around North Beach in his tennis shoes, started

7

hanging out at a bar named Pistola's. He had sold his interest in the Golden Eagle bar and thought he was out of the saloon business, but the possibilities of the space intrigued him, especially when the owner, Rose Evangelista, said she was ready to retire.

In 1973, Sam and Ed paid $25,000 for the bar, in partnership with two other North Beach bar owners, and they were in business. They had purchased the rights to a long, narrow, drink dungeon with blacked out windows. The rent was $300 a month. As homage to the former owner, a rose was included on new signage and had enduring significance.

The renovation was placed in the hands of San Francisco architects and twin brothers, Tom and Ted Eden, who reportedly accepted the task for a nominal sum and a year's worth of free food and booze. An attractive makeover of Pistola's could have been accomplished, but it's hard to imagine a space shaped like a bocce ball court, would have generated the bar, restaurant, entertainment, and legend, that evolved. Too small. Fortunately, an adjacent commercial space, a tropical fish store next door, became available. The former neighbor made for many silly jokes when diners asked about fresh fish. *Poached tetra with lemon aioli sauce?*

Sam's appreciation for New York saloons set the style template for WSB&G: What had been the Pistola side was dominated by a French walnut bar of the classic San Francisco style, found at an architectural salvage business, along with nine linen draped tables. The piscatorial side, with 22 tables, was separated from the raucous atmosphere of the bar, by a load-bearing wall, which was open at each end, with heavy curtains that could be drawn to create a more intimate dining experience. However, feelings of camaraderie, people watching, and being part of the action, not intimate dining, were the attractions at WSB&G. The curtains were seldom drawn.

The two rooms were pulled together by a wide frieze painted in a reddish, earthy color artists call *burnt sienna*. Black and white photos, with white mats and black frames, were displayed on the frieze. The upper walls and ceiling were painted a buff color. Two large mirrors, one behind the bar and the other above an upright piano, helped create an illusion of spaciousness. Insofar as the décor was determined by Sam, it reflected his personality: Uncluttered, straight forward, and confident of being judged on its own merit.

The atmosphere the trio hoped to create was based on their favorite hangouts in New York City, particularly Artists and Writers restaurant, where bright, literate people went to dine and be served by bright and literate people. If they at least accomplished that, they figured they'd have an enjoyable hangout for themselves.

For all the visual attempts to create the appearance of spaciousness, WSB&G was impossibly small. The kitchen, outfitted with an industrial range covered with burners, and surmounted by shelves piled high with sauté pans, could only accommodate two cooks. Adjacent to the hot kitchen was a tiny space with refrigerator cabinets and shelves where one person made salads and cold appetizers. Nearby was a dishwashing area stuck into a cul-de-sac in a wall. Logistics said the food prep areas couldn't possibly have produced the volume of meals that it did.

The remaining space, where food servers had to operate, was a rabbit warren of refrigerators, cubicles, tiny closets, and cramped aisles. When human bodies were added, close proximity was an understatement. The traditional alert "behind you" which is how waiters signal to each other that they're passing with arms full of plates, was a near constant refrain.

Adjacent to the kitchen doors, were the restrooms, which recalled the days when such were called "water closets" and closets were small. The women's room eventually had a cosmetic upgrade with wallpaper and a bit of paint. But, if one sat on the toilet and closed the door, their knees would be under their chin. Size-wise, WSB&G was a biscotti box trying to be a restaurant.

In the hierarchy of responsibilities, Sam was in charge of the rickety infrastructure, which was an extension of a rickety neighborhood, and therefore beset with unfixable problems. But, Sam relished the role of Duct Tape Engineer-in-Chief. The state of the electrical wiring was frightening to contemplate. When the power went out, Sam would instruct the staff to get out candles and carry on. When the ancient plumbing refused to cooperate, Sam would walk around chortling, "Surf's up, gang!"

The rest of the time, Sam meticulously monitored the decrepit set up for house cleaning chores. He flicked away near invisible motes of dust and demanded waiters scrupulously empty ashtrays at the first appearance of a cigarette butt. In off peak hours, the wait staff better look busy sweeping, cleaning, polishing, and organizing.

One of my early employers, Norman Gilbert, who was a genius chef and amiable alcoholic, passed along a useful tip he learned as an apprentice. He said, "I always carried a hammer, so it looked like I'd just fixed something or was on the way to." I adapted that to give Sam the impression I was a paragon of diligence. Sam being Sam, he probably didn't buy it, but appreciated the ploy.

After purchasing Pistola's and setting up a semi-workable operation, attracting customers became the focus. Sam, Ed, and Mary Etta, had the usual strikes against them; new place, unknown commodity, and suspicion, as newcomers to a neighborhood set in its ways. They purchased an upright piano and hired jazz talent to enliven the evenings. But, it wasn't working until an unlikely person named Glenn Dorenbush took an interest in the new place.

Glenn was a publicist of the kind only San Francisco could produce. He claimed his job was "sitting on barstools." He was a red-faced, shuffling figure whose straight, dark, chin-length hair looked as though his stylist was an Amish woman with scissors and a bowl. He spoke through barely parted teeth and his heavy eyelids were usually half closed. His sleep-walking appearance belied a keen wit and breadth of education acquired in college and law school.

He started chatting up Washington Square Bar & Grill to his friends and media contacts, notably Herb Caen, the *San Francisco Chronicle*'s premiere columnist. Herb's daily column full of juicy tidbits, society gossip, quirks and foibles of his beloved city, was must-read material with morning coffee for much of the Bay Area.

Early on, I sent Herb an item—and worried at my presumption. I noted a business in the Richmond district called Hinton Peck, taught dance, not typing. Herb, who typed his columns on an archaic manual typewriter, printed it with attribution and gave it "full marks." Ed was mystified and asked if Dorenbush submitted it for me. (Naïve though I was, I could see that Herb's column required a constant deluge from multiple sources.) The next time Dorenbush came in, he cast his bleary eyes in my direction and raised a thumbs up.

For news consumers in the post-Herb Caen era (newspapers are no longer a given) the columnist's influence cannot be explained. He created a niche for himself in a form originated by legendary news man, Walter Winchell, called an "items column." Snippets and observations were separated by elipses, or as Herb termed it "three dot journalism."

What Herb said became gospel for the masses, such as his decision that "Frisco" was unseemly for the city he termed "Baghdad by the Bay" and, henceforth, must always be spoken of long form as San Francisco. Everyone, in a city famous for non-conformity, obediently pronounced all the extra syllables.

When I became a columnist at *The Oakland Tribune*, I resurrected Frisco. That raised a how-dare-you ruckus on both sides of the water. I knew Herb had confessed he regretted the name change. He was amused at my across-the-Estuary tweak, and gave the silliness a wink.

Herb called the new, up-and-coming place "the Washbag." Coulda been worse, I quipped, like "the Deitschbag." However, no one, who worked at Washington Square Bar & Grill, liked Herb's Washbag contraction. Instead, we called it "The Square." Looking back at all my clever colleagues, I'm surprised something more ingenious wasn't coined, but we went with expediency.

When Ron Fimrite, who was a well-known sports writer and devoted patron, was researching a book about Washington Square Bar & Grill, I was stingy with my stories, but noted the staff used The Square not Washbag. I recall he was surprised at the in-house term and revamped his plans for the book's title.

In this account, I will not use Washbag or The Square. No how-dare-you ruckus needed. Rather, I'll pay tribute to the ampersand by using the full name of my decades-long place of employment or just WSB&G. While many people were familiar with the typographic character back then, I daresay, few recognized the word *ampersand*, which is remarkable considering how long the squiggle has been part of written language. It appeared as graffiti on the walls of Pompeii and in the writings of Marcus Aurelius.

Did Lawrence "Larry" Green have that history in mind when he created the distinctive logo of WSB&G? The graphics designer usually had his glasses stuck in his rumpled hair and his handsome face had a harried look, as though he was perpetually on deadline. Given his many projects and talents as a designer, illustrator, cartoonist, and inventor, harried may have been the case. Green could have worked from any part of the City, but preferred North Beach, and set up his studio in several neighborhood locations. That was also handy for visiting one of his most active accounts.

Green's design concept for Washington Square Bar & Grill used a graceful version of the ampersand for all print and billboard designs, for business cards, matchbooks, and menus. He incorporated the ampersand into whimsical cartoon figures: A waiter pouring coffee from an ampersand pot. A society lady with an ampersand coif on her head. A chef with an ampersand on a platter. Every year, Green added to the cartoon ampersand family and his boundless ingenuity was anticipated when the new designs were unveiled.

Prior to Green's use of the ampersand, I don't recall seeing it anywhere. Now it's positively ubiquitous. Similarly, Bar & Grill was a new coinage. Now it's everywhere. Imitation being the sincerest form of flattery, Larry Green should have his own wing in the Flattery Hall of Fame.

& without further ado, here's more of the story…

2

Rashomon & Wild Rabbits

I n the 1950 film, *Rashomon,* director Akira Kurosawa presented four different accounts of a murder and explored the subjective nature of truth. Thereafter, the term *Rashomon Effect* became shorthand for one event that can generate numerous perspectives. Washington Square Bar & Grill was Rashomon, or given the Italian influence of North Beach, Rashomonetti or Rashomonino.

The Rashomon reference may seem wildly dated. Really, 1950? In the filmography of actors like Keanu Reeves or Tom Cruise, there may be more updated versions of the Rashomon Effect, but the Kurosawa film, stamped with the magnetism of the great Japanese actor, Toshiro Mifune, established the Dagwood sandwich of realities that is Rashomon.

The variety of WSB&G's allure and attractions provided ample Rashomon material for people to stack up personal perceptions. Each person had treasured memories and impressions, which may have been influenced by the time of day, the day of the week, reports in the media, their partying pals, the music and food, and the famous extra-curricular activities.

While the hectic power lunches and busy dinner hours accounted for many impressions, there was quiet time for tippling and friend meetups in the afternoon. A televised sports' event could bring together fans in a raucous sports' bar atmosphere. Jazz concerts drew appreciative fans. The stylings of accomplished pianists enhanced the evening hours. During Sunday brunch, with dappled sunlight streaming through the windows, the ambiance was conducive to pleasant conversations, reading the voluminous *Chronicle/Examiner* Sunday edition, or working the crossword puzzles of the *New York Times.*

The most remarkable feature of WSB&G may have been that an individual could stop in for an adult beverage and very likely have an adult conversation. While many of the City's bars were "meat markets," aglow with fake Tiffany lamps in low light gloom, where the air was thick with raging hormones and desperate hope, WSB&G was an oasis from hustle and sexual come-ons. The customer base, which in large part was literate and amusing, knew and respected that.

Conversation was still prized in the days before the home entertainment industry turned living spaces into cocoons and Amazon delivered the world to one's doorstep. Human contact still had to be sought out and WSB&G could usually deliver someone worth talking to.

On the weekends, the curious from outside the City limits descended on WSB&G to see what all the fuss was about. Business folks from the Financial District shed their three-piece suits and wing tips, to show up in alligator shirts and Reeboks. Yuppies was the generic term applied to the young shirt-and-tie crowd, and the multiple layers of enjoyment of WSB&G seemed lost on them. A fellow named, Jay and his crowd were Yuppies, who dined frequently. Jay liked really cold butter for the sourdough bread. As soon as I saw him arrive, I would put a ramekin of butter in the freezer for a quick chill down, and would deliver it to him even if another waiter was serving him.

Jay's cold butter quirk was the only thing noteworthy about him and his companions. They didn't converse much among themselves. They may have been celebrity-seeking, but I suspect their frame of celebrity references was limited. They were just there. It takes all kinds to fill a restaurant. But, there was a covert fear that Yuppies and hollow-at-the-core money men would eventually control the City and muscle out the colorful, wacky, artistic element that had long given San Francisco its unique character.

At all times, customers found menu items that were tasty, substantial, and determined by Mary Etta Moose, the resident foodie. She kept an eye on the exciting developments in California cuisine that were coming from Alice Waters' restaurant, Chez Panisse, in Berkeley and tracked the Waters' acolytes, who were spreading their wings. While Mary Etta tapped into the new cuisine for specials, WSB&G fare never became too experimental, fussy, or precious.

The products Mary Etta purchased were always top quality: Sourdough bread from Parisian Bakery. Pates from Marcel et Henri charcuterie. Sacripantina, delicate layers of white cake and crème in glass cups from Stella pastries. Chocolate Decadence, a flourless chocolate torte baked by neighborhood woman and topped with house made whipped cream. Coffee, a special blend of light and dark, from Graffeo roastery. Ice cream from Double Rainbow. (The spumoni was irresistible and many waiters carried a spoon to dip a taste for themselves when filling an order.) Veal and beef for scallopini and speidini had to be the best. Petrale and Rex sole fresh off the boats. And, the pasta, mmmm, *Mama mia!*

Seasonable favorites from the East Coast, like shad roe and softshell crabs, were flown in. Preferred customers were advised, placed their orders, and showed up with forks at-the-ready when the shipments arrived. Likewise, specially ordered bottles of Beaujolais Nouveau were cause for celebrations.

Food costs, Sam claimed, were one of the reasons why WSB&G, despite doing voluminous business, didn't show great profits. But, once a standard of excellence in food quality has been set, it's considered unwise to try to cut corners. The profit margins in all restaurants are slim and require heads up management. Having jumped into a deal for Pistola's, the partners may not have laid out a long-term business plan, but were stuck with what they had. As the quip goes "The only thing worse than failure is success."

Supposedly, Ed sweated the small stuff. Considering the breadth of his need to control, it's hard to imagine he didn't give a nod to food costs, although nominally that was someone else's responsibility. And, bean counting didn't have the wow-factor he relished. Undoubtedly, though, his greatest attribute was public relations and seeing possibilities in small things that became big things when the force of his personality was added. That was the case with the Penny Pitching Contest.

Apparently, the game of tossing coins against a wall is as old as coins (the winner's coin falls closest to the wall) and was favored by poor people in cities as far back as ancient Greece. It was popularized, and bet on, by the working classes in 19th century Britain, and known to American city kids. So, when Ed was strolling to work and saw his maître d' Hal Thunes and a few others pitching pennies against the walls of WSB&G, he recognized the game and quickly saw potential for an event.

The location at 1707 Powell Street, in a triangle between Columbus Avenue to the east and Union Street on the west, was beneficial in having several parking places and a short stretch of connecting thoroughfare that could be blocked off for special events.

Before long, Ed was filling up the space with Penny Pitching teams of WSB&G regulars, celebrities, and sports' figures, competing in fundraisers for Ed's favorite charity, St. Anthony's Dining Room.

While waiting on celebrities that participated in Penny Pitching, Sofi Kurtz and Marcy Campagne, who were big sports' fans, met San Francisco 49ers, Dwight Hicks and Charley Young. The footballers had so much fun, they returned with their wives to meet the two engaging waitresses. The meetup didn't end there. Sometime later, Joe Montana was having dinner at WSB&G, and the two goof-balls wrote a note to Hicks and Young, and asked the famous 49er Quarterback to deliver it. (No Instagram or Facebook in those days.)

After work, the twosome went to Perry's for a drink and there again was Joe Montana, who, by that time, was skeptical about play-ing postman. Well acquainted with how women throw themselves at athletes, Joe said he wasn't comfortable delivering a note without knowing the contents. Marcy assured him it had nothing to do with a Motel 6 hookup, explained the circumstances, and invited him to read it. Says Marcy "I thought Joe showed real integrity."

Happenstance arising from everyday events, like the Penny Pitch, also gave birth to Ed's most famous creation, his globe-trotting, hard-drinking, sometimes hard-hitting, softball team which came to be called *Les Lapins Sauvages*. The phenomenon began in 1978 as a casual get-together of old jocks at the North Beach playground where Joe DiMaggio played as a youngster. The game was so popular with the participants, they were soon ready to go beyond intramural competition and seek out other opponents. Their first serious rival was Cookie Picetti's Star Buffet on Kearny Street.

That dive bar, adjacent to the old Court House, was popu-lated by cops and robbers, that is to say, the staff needed to run a legal system. Bail bondsmen, lawyers, parolees, defendants, past and present residents of the crow bar hotel, and law enforcement, all frequented Cookie's. He was owner and bartender. His long, mournful-looking face, punctuated with a cigar, belied the drollness required to run such a place. The restrooms were labeled *Hung Jury* and *Split Decision.*

To contest Ed's team, Cookie assembled a squad of cops that delivered a serious drubbing to the saloon dilettantes. The defeat stoked Ed's fervent need to be The Winner. He began assembling a team that would serve his various agendas. From the media, he recruited sports' writers, Ron Fimrite and David Bush, along with Herb Caen, who could all ballyhoo the teams' travels.

From Cookie's team, Ed attracted Chris Sullivan, a jovial, red-faced Irish cop, who related to me one of his proudest moments. In 1977, two rival gangs with Hong Kong roots, the Joe Boys and the Wah Ching, had a deadly shootout at a Chinatown restaurant that was called the Golden Dragon Massacre. While the gang members were known to police, they were at large for a time. Chris's cop radar was triggered when he spotted one of the suspects trying to blend in on a Chinatown street. Said Chris, "I knew it was him. I just knew." Cuffs on.

Sullivan was a beloved WSB&G regular, popular with the staff and the ladies. He earned his slot on the team, like pianist Dick Fregulia and actor-turned businessman, Claude Jarman, because of athletic ability. Lawyers, stock-brokers, bankers, rounded out the roster.

There were persistent rumors that Ed sneaked in "ringers" semi-professional ball players to bolster his chances. He always professed his players had to be "over 40 or have a bad liver," a mantra that was relentlessly repeated. However, playing ball with Ed brought together people from all walks of life, as did WSB&G.

Investment banker, Herbert Allen, Jr. whose portfolio included Coca Cola and Columbia Pictures, was an unlikely team regular, who could afford to jet in on his own plane for a game anywhere anytime. He and Ed were said to be polar opposites in many ways, but had a convivial friendship. Having the wherewithal to participate in Ed's expanding schedule of away games must have been a problem for some players. Travel and lodging expenses were significant, but probably paled compared to the bar tabs.

The first foray out of San Francisco was a game against Steven Spurrier's restaurant, Le Moulin du Village, in Paris. Spurrier, a Brit, was an internationally known wine expert, writer, merchant, and educator, who had given California wines an incredible boost when he entered several California selections into a prestigious 1976 blind tasting in Paris—and the NorCal grapes won.

Owing to Spurrier's frequent trips to California wine country and Ed's globe-trotting to Paris and Rome, the two got together often for wining and dining. During one of their long lunches, Spurrier and Ed cooked up the idea of an intra-restaurant softball game on the Bois du Bologne. Was *Sitting Duck* on the menu? Spurrier's team probably had cricket or soccer experience, but softball was unfamiliar, just the kind of competition Ed appreciated.

On the transatlantic flight to France, an omission was corrected. The WSB&G team didn't have an official name, but someone's fractured French came up with *Les Lapins Sauvages*. Aiming for The Wild Hares (a play on A Wild Hair?) the soft ballers were, instead, Wild Rabbits.

The Paris excursion was the first of many destinations. Central Park in NYC, Fenway Park, Wrigley Field, Yankee stadium, and England-Ireland trip, Hong Kong, and Moscow followed. Like an autocratic chaperone for a kiddie field trip, Ed made all the decisions, except for late-night hotel trysts and bed-hopping Bingo.

The soft-ballers often glimpsed what the general public didn't see, Ed's need for absolute control, his tantrums, grudges, and the mercurial darkness that would overtake him. A bad play on the ball field could set him off. Any small success by an opposing team was bitterly resented. Instead of shaking it off, Ed would pace and stomp and mutter. To the competitors, softball was just fun, just a day at the park, just reliving the days of youth, just camaraderie. To Ed it was war.

Writing in *Image Magazine* in 1986, Bill Cardosa related a characteristic incident:

"Scorekeeper Patsy Glynn also knows fear of Moose. Patsy, at 103 tough pounds is a feisty trial lawyer who goes for the jugular. 'Hey, Moose! Don't take anybody out!' she advised [during a game with Columbia Pictures in Encino.]

"Moose rushed over, jabbing a finger, pulling himself up to his full six-feet-three, glaring imperiously. "You are the scorer!" he roared masterfully at the pitiful, shrinking litigator. 'Whereas I, I am the manager!"

Ron Fimrite dusted Ed's bad temperament with confectioner's sugar, claiming Ed was just emulating the fierce coaching tactics of Leo Durocher. Uh, huh. And Caligula was a Billy Martin wannabe. Amazingly, a group that included high-performing professionals, tolerated the abusive outbursts. When players occasionally quit the team, it was because they felt they were unfairly warming the bench, not because they were treated like Joan Crawford's kids.

All of his "close" associates noted Ed's complexity. But how close were they? How deeply did they inquire? Not very much, I'm sure. And, not surprisingly. Men from that era didn't give group hugs. Impossible to imagine that Ron Fimrite or Claude Jarman or Herb Caen or any of the softball teammates would take Ed aside to discuss his mood swings, his feelings, or the tumultuous state of his chakras. *Hey, big guy, I see your mellow is a little out of balance. Wanna talk?*

No, Ed was the conductor of the Fun Train, not a spiritual leader. Sharing inner thoughts would have been a buzz kill for the Lapins. Sam, who was not one for mawkish PDAs, was unlikely to interface with his partner for a sensitivity session. So, in that man-to-man realm, Ed was probably on his own. Although he had a masters' degree in sociology, that's an area of study, which seems to fall pretty low on the physician-heal-thyself list.

Not only was Ed a softball coach, he was the ringmaster at the City's most popular gathering place. His life of saloons, cronies, good food, strong drinks, politics, back-slapping and laughs was enviable to many. So why the dark clouds?

Perhaps, Ed Moose also suffered from Not Enough. He had great intellect, creativity, resourcefulness, leadership, charm, wit, the whole package to do anything and to succeed. He was friends with captains of industry, political heavyweights, celebrities, sports legends, and local luminaries. But, when the drinks had all been quaffed, when the daily measure of laughter and male-bonding concluded, those people went back to real jobs. Ed's job was running a bar.

His variant of Not Enough manifested as Never Enough. Attention, public acclaim, power, fame, control, celebrity friends, travel—all of that, it seems, was Never Enough.

I spent years working in upscale restaurants and bars. I love bars, from posh to neighborhood to biker. But, I knew it couldn't be my endgame. While I took my time exiting the bar business, I didn't want to be Lucy Kendall.

A tiny, feisty, old woman, Lucy had given her life to the labor movement. She supplemented her retirement income by serving brunch at WSB&G. She was slow, inefficient, and easily flustered. Customers, who didn't know her backstory or the special circumstance of her employment, could be harsh. We did our best to protect her and take up the slack. But, if I didn't find something else to do, I could see myself in the same situation. I was determined to remain single and answerable only to myself, which complicated my prospects.

All bars, even the highly successful ones, are gin mill Potemkin villages where the façade of conviviality melts in the morning light. Waitress Sofi Kurtz knew that. Olive skinned, with exotic good looks, she was an intense, transplanted New Yorker, who had degrees from Smith and Cornell. She trained and had practiced as a psychiatric social worker, but her unofficial practice at WSB&G was devoted to commenting on the ample idiosyncrasies of the staff and customers. Her informative and near constant analysis was our elevator music.

Sofi also understood the *empty calories* nature of the bar business. She shrewdly said "You can only leave the Washington Square Bar & Grill, when you accept that life will never again be as much fun."

Ed must have known that, too. He was trapped in his own Rashomon Effect, a serious man, a former do-gooder, floating on ephemera. He couldn't leave. He'd staked his fortune on the saloon. Nor could he accept life less fun. Too many fun-seekers depended on him. Those realizations, added to what may have been a sense of his own failed potential, and sluiced with Catholic guilt, made Ed's stroboscopic personality more understandable.

Besides softball, Ed's other enthusiasm was politics, true blue Democrat, of course. His name-dropping suggested he was chummy with every Big Name Dem. When exasperated with WSB&G, he threatened "to go work for Bill Bradley." (No word if Bradley unplugged his phone.) However, Ed had been a campaign director for liberal presidential candidate Fred Harris, who has gone down in history as Fred Who?

The campaigner connection may be why Ed hired Maya Luckmann, who was at loose ends after working on Tom Hayden's unsuccessful 1976 primary campaign for senator. Maya, who worked as a hostess at WSB&G, epitomized the over qualified nature of much of the staff. She spoke in deliciously complicated sentences that I appreciated, as a Baby Boomer, who had diagrammed sentences on the blackboard, the more so as English was not her first language.

Maya was born in Yugoslavia, educated in Germany, and sought a master's degree in sociology at Rutgers University. She was following in the footsteps of her distinguished father, Thomas Luckmann, an internationally recognized professor of sociology. With her master's degree studies nearly completed, Maya decamped for California. She had an abiding interest in trade unionism and progressive politics, but set that aside temporarily for a stint at WSB&G.

As a hostess, she often worked with Hal Thunes and there was great fondness between the two of them. Hal called her "My Little Magyar." Probably grateful for an American with a smidge of interest in European history, Maya never told Hal that Magyars are Hungarian, not Yugoslavian.

In 1979, Maya left WSB&G for a job as Education Director for Local 2, Hotel and Restaurant Union at its Tenderloin office, but we remained friends and adventure seekers. Four decades later, we both recall a disturbing incident, but define it in different terms. We planned to attend a midnight screening of *The Rocky Horror Picture Show* at a theater on Market Street, which was an iffy location back then. I found a parking spot about two blocks from the theater and we walked along a dark, seemingly empty sidewalk.

Suddenly, a homeless person materialized from the darkness and attacked us. We both screamed and flailed our arms and the attacker disappeared back into the murk. Maya, despite her egghead credentials, was more streetwise than I was, chose to call it "an encounter."

I chose to internalize it as a warning of female vulnerability. In a time of burgeoning feminism, the encounter was a reminder that safety is not a given. The only other direct incident I had with a homeless person was in North Beach. Co-worker, Gary Epting, offered to walk me to my car at the end of our shift. We passed a bag lady, who had been hanging around the neighborhood. Previously, we had given her money and considered her harmless. That night, she had a psychotic meltdown and began screaming and beating us.

Of course, aggressive pan-handling could be expected in those days at various places that could be avoided, but current reports of homeless encampments all over San Francisco, whose filth and disorder go unchecked, are the hardest images to reconcile with a once graceful city. The additional peril for women of unhinged, drug-addicted, homeless men and the restrictions to women's free movements, are distressing.

When Maya was hired at Local 2, her particular focus was women and minority workers. The union was just emerging from a leadership shake-up and a strike against the City's union hotels in 1980 that highlighted the industry bias in favor of hiring men. The settlement of the strike failed to dislodge the prejudice against hiring women and minorities and allowed 12 top hotel restaurants to continue ignoring affirmative action and seniority guidelines.

When Maya and I socialized, we didn't talk shop. I respected the work she was doing, but failed to appreciate the larger implications. My mindset about trade unionism was stuck on Pete Seeger, twanging on his banjo, and singing Which Side Are You On?"

Of course, my co-workers at WSB&G, doing menial work like washing dishes and bussing tables, needed union protection. We valued them and didn't consider them expendable, but management might. I naively thought college educations and restaurant skills, which many of us had, was a quasi-firewall against a throwaway mentality. Surely the staff members with outstanding personalities, doing quality work, attracting their own followings, contributing substantially to the company coffers, surely, they were exempt from capricious firings by an autocratic boss, weren't they?

3

"There must be somebody here!"

Celebrities began appearing in my life very early. That was improbable given the blue collar, making-ends-meet nature of our family, which lived in unpretentious Rivera Beach, Florida. However, my father, Arthur Berkley, worked at the Palm Beach Country Club on nearby Palm Beach island, which has long been a playground of the rich and famous.

The development of that golf course, situated on the north end of the island between Lake Worth and the Atlantic Ocean, began in 1915 when famous course designer, Donald Ross, started drafting the layout. By the mid-1950s, the property and a hotel became a private Jewish club, because wealthy Jews found themselves excluded from the Everglades, Bath and Tennis club, and other swanky Palm Beach spots.

My father was the manager of the men's locker room, a feature of most golf courses where members change from street clothes and shoes into golfing attire. That position is usually menial and unremarkable, but Dad was such a sparkplug of hustle and hospitality, he became somewhat well-known among wealthy East Coast golfers. Dad used to say, "If you're a good worker, you can always get a job."

His job was done so well, the members of Palm Beach Country Club could tell their guests from business, politics, entertainment, high society, and sports, that "Arthur" would take good care of them. They could be assured that a red carpet would be rolled out for the visitors, which reflected well on them. Dad kept an autograph book on hand as a keepsake for me, so I was meeting celebrities for years—on paper. A few of the names in my autograph book indicate the variety of guests at PBCC: Bing Crosby, Tony Curtis, golfers Sam Snead and Julius Boros, politician Abe Ribicoff, Israeli diplomat and politician Abba Eban, Edward Duke of Windsor, and John F. Kennedy.

As an Irish Catholic, Joseph Kennedy, was not admitted into the hallowed halls of Palm Beach society. However, Palm Beach Country Club accepted him as a member. The Kennedy family's ocean front home was nearby and Dad said he "watched the kids grow up."

One day in the early 1960s, he hastily called Mom and told her to bring me and my brother to the club. The president, John F. Kennedy, was going to be teeing off for a round of golf. Dad was diligent about glimpses of history for his kids. In 1955, when he was working a summer job at the Mt. Washington Hotel in New Hampshire, he rushed home to our rented cottage, and gathered us to see President Dwight D. Eisenhower, who was speaking at Franconia Notch.

President Kennedy arrived for his tee time in a Lincoln convertible. Secret Servicemen, carrying golf bags with no clubs, stationed themselves along the fairway. His hair tousled by the sea breeze, JFK hit a booming drive that sliced and hit a serviceman in the head. The rules of golf were a bit unclear, so the president, after waving an apology, took a mulligan.

One of my earliest experiences with the perks of privilege came when I briefly dated an aide to the Kennedys. We were parked, in the same Lincoln, out by the beach on South Ocean Boulevard, talking and watching the moonlight on the waves. A cop rolled up on us and asked for the aide's ID, which he consulted with a flashlight. He walked around the Lincoln, surveyed the license plate, and backed away apologizing.

Dad was able to arrange for me to attend a presidential press conference at The Breakers Hotel conducted by Pierre Salinger. I was contemplating a journalism major in college, edited my high school newspaper, and briefly had a "school news" column in the Palm Beach Post newspaper. I dressed for the occasion, in Jackie Kennedy-influenced style, a navy blue knit dress, high heels, pillbox hat, and white gloves. Around my neck was a string of red and white *pop beads,* a plastic jewelry fad that would have horrified Jackie.

I took a seat in the conference room and noted the professional journalists, who were mostly unshaven, dressed in Bermuda shorts, and Hawaiian shirts, and casually draped over the furniture. I sat upright in my chair, as young ladies of the time were instructed, and clasped my hands over the purse in my lap. At the conclusion of his remarks, Pierre Salinger approached me and said "You must be Arthur's daughter." I was surprised at the recognition and thought "How could he know that?"

How indeed? Sore thumb?

My journalism plans fell victim to Not Enough. I would be the first in my family to attend college. For a blue-collar kid to aspire to journalism seemed presumptuous. I decided to be a teacher.

My Dad's service to Palm Beach Country Club members went so far as telling super rich people to get in touch with me if they happened to be in Boston or Aspen or San Francisco or wherever I had fetched up. Amazingly, some did. A wealthy, married couple that manufactured children's clothing, contacted Arthur's daughter, who was then a college drop-out and ski bum in Aspen. The husband, who was a more advanced skier, hired me to keep his wife company on the bunny hills. Being paid to ski was a dream come true.

Ski bum attire in those days, born of indigence and anti-fashion attitudes, was jeans over thermal underwear, a couple layers on top, plus a goose down vest purchased if one had a financial windfall. When Madam Ski Bunny asked me whether she should wear her lynx parka or her antelope parka, I knew I was going to be earning my pay.

Another traveler sent by my Dad was a high-ranking official in the Four Seasons Hotel chain. In 1978, that corporation acquired the Clift Hotel, one of San Francisco's grand old hotels, which was venerated by locals for its backbar. Those massive, carved, wooden structures, usually mirrored, stood against walls and held liquor bottles, glassware, and supplies. Among serious saloon aficionados, a beautiful, historic backbar like the carved rosewood and birch structure at the Temple Bar on Tillman Place, was reason enough for a visit.

The backbar of the Redwood Room at the Clift Hotel was iconic, supposedly carved from a single 800-year-old redwood tree. Customers at the front bar could rest their elbows on a long brass rail supported in the trunks of brass African elephants with ears aflair.

Dining at the Clift was equally posh and the gentleman referred by Dad, who I'll call the Generous Host, invited me, and a date, to join him for an evening of no limits wining and dining. I brought Brian St. Pierre, who was public relations director of the Wine Institute and a food and wine writer. He could hardly wait to study the Clift's voluminous wine list. After cocktails, appetizers, and get-acquainted chatting, the wine list was presented. Our Generous Host indicated to the waiter that Brian would do the selecting, then commented that he didn't like wine.

Brian took this as a personal challenge and offered to order wines that would change our Generous Host's mind. I could see two of them were getting on famously, so it was a good time for a powder room break. The super-rich, I learned, do not use public restrooms. Generous Host handed me the keys to the penthouse on the 17th floor, which was always reserved for his visits, and told me to relax and enjoy.

After sprucing up, I boarded the elevator. The doors opened at a lower floor, and Arnold Schwarzenegger with a bodacious redhead, entered. Proper etiquette for sharing an elevator with strangers is always problematic. Nod in acknowledgment? Stare at the floor?

Pretending Arnold was invisible seemed silly. He was already well-known for *Pumping Iron*, the documentary that introduced the Austrian-born body builder and his sport to a world-wide audience. The Conan movies had furthered his recognizability. So, I said "Hello, Arnold."

Big mistake. Arnold's head snapped in my direction. His eyes drilled on my face. His massive square jaw ground forward and he hissed "Howissitdatchuknowme?"

The indecipherable utterance combined with his menacing Terminator look was perplexing—and downright scary. When I didn't answer, he repeated, with more emphasis "Howissitdatchuknowme?"

What was he saying? German for How dare you speak to me? Austrian colloquialism for You are less than schnitzel to me? I shifted nervously back and forth waiting for the elevator door to open, but still he continued, and followed me into the lobby saying "Howissitdatchuknowme?"

I sprinted ahead and hid behind a potted palm until he left.

The mysterious episode, which seemed so fraught with menace, was explained the next day. I was watching "People Are Talking" which was a popular morning talk show on KPIX TV that was hosted by Ann Fraser and Ross McGowan. Arnold Schwarzenegger was the featured guest. During the interview, Arnold explained to Ross that he was managing his own business affairs, including market research to determine which of his enterprises, whether films or body building, or something else, were reaching people.

Ross asked "How do you do that?"

Arnold replied "Ven I meet peepo, I ask dem How issit dat chu know me?"

The parade of celebrities that passed through Washington Square Bar & Grill, was part of its lore. Passersby on the sidewalk would peer in the windows to see who might be there. When something noteworthy was going on, like the 1984 Democrat convention, gawkers would be mobbed up outside the windows. While I respect the work and achievements that result in becoming a high-profile figure, I was somewhat immune to crazed fandom because I'd already met the biggest star in my cosmos.

In 1968, I was working at the Rams Head Inn at Killington, Vermont, which was a cozy, old-style lodge decorated with snow-shoes and bear trap skis on the walls. There was a lounge area with a fireplace, a small bar, and a dining room where everyone ate more or less the same time. One of the guests was Bob Beattie, who was the founder of the U.S. Ski Team, coach of Olympic alpine skiers, a life-long big deal in skiing, and a delightful gentleman. He joined in the nightly routine that brought together the entire staff, indeed the whole world, watching the TV coverage of the Winter Olympics in Grenoble, France.

The great French ski racer, Jean-Claude Killy, had been tearing up the competition prior to Grenoble, and was thought to be a triple medalist contender, the second since Austrian skier, Tony Sailer, won in 1956. Everyone at Rams Head Inn was a skier, from the dishwashers to the owners, so we all squeezed into the lounge, to witness history. The coverage was in black and white and the final event, the downhill, was problematic as fog rolled in and Killy was accused of missing a gate. In the end, the handsome, charismatic Killy was awarded three golds.

The following winter, I was ski bumming in Aspen. I had saved enough money to buy a ski pass at Aspen Highlands. On a glorious, sparkling day, with money in my pocket I rode the shuttle bus from town out to the Highlands. Then, ski pass around my neck and feeling top of the world, I bought a hot chocolate and walked out to a deck that overlooked the ski slope.

A figure sitting at a table waved to me and yelled "Judy, come join me." It was Bob Beattie. After a bit of chit chat, I said "What are you doing here, Bob?"

He said he was providing support for Jean-Claude Killy, who was in Aspen filming TV commercials. At that moment, a figure was descending the slope, carving serpentine turns in our direction. He skidded to a stop, in a shower of glittering snow crystals—right in front of us. It was Killy.

In charming French-accented English, the living legend said "Bob, we are finished filming for the day."

Beattie turned to me and said "Do you need a ride into town?"

If I had driven a vintage Rolls Royce to the Highlands, I still would have said "Yes, YES, I need a ride!"

Killy rode shotgun, Beattie drove, and I sat in the backseat. The gold medalist, the biggest thing in skiing, an international mega star, twisted in his seat to chat with me about life in Aspen. In terms of celebrity encounters, it never got better than that. It got pretty good, but never better.

Thanks to Herb Caen's column, Washington Square Bar & Grill became so famous as a place for celebrity-spotting that out-of-towners and weekend suburbanites from the East Bay had the notion that a recognizable A-B-C Lister of some sort was always on site. Now, the staff was, in fact, protective of celebrity privacy and not likely to point out any public figures, who might be dining. The star-seekers assumed that was the case and were sure that wheedling their waiter incessantly would worm out an identity because "There must be somebody here!"

It got so tiresome, I started making up celebrities. An older fellow from the neighborhood helped me out with the deception. Charlie had a full head of white hair in a brush cut. He was my stand-in for actor George C. Scott. Charlie sat at the bar drinking Heinekin beers and when I was pointing him out as George C, he would smile and tip the green bottle at the gawkers.

Another time, I read in Herb's column that actor Richard Dreyfuss was in the city. When pests demanded a celebrity, I looked around the room for someone vaguely fitting Dreyfuss' description. That satisfied them, but got sketchy when the real Richard Dreyfuss walked through the door.

A customer noticed a person at an adjacent table was actor George Wendt from the TV sitcom *Cheers*. He was overcome with excitement ("It's Norm, oh, my God, it's Norm!") and demanded I get an autograph for him. I refused to be a proxy autograph hound. The customer became nasty and insisted. I leaned into the guy, lowered my voice and said "For Pete's sake, man, it's George Wendt, not Laurence Olivier."

I figured my admonishment would cost me a tip. Inexplicably, the guy left me $100.

There was a time that a celebrity had to be pointed out to me. John Wasserman was the *Chronicle*'s film critic, an affable guy, who loved a window table and therefore was one of my regulars. One afternoon, he arrived an hour before dinner service started. From the large Family Table at the back of the dining room where the staff was having our evening meal, I saw John at the front door, walked up, greeted him there, and explained food service wouldn't begin for a while.

He looked back to the Family Table and asked if he could eat with us. He offered to pay. Of course, we couldn't allow that. So, he was our guest, an enjoyable dinner companion, who joined in our usual banter. Thus, when John appeared in my station a few days later, I was focused on seeing him again.

He said "Judy, I want you to meet someone…" I turned to his companion whose square jaw, green eyes, and shock of brown hair, were faintly familiar. John finished the intro, "This is Clint Eastwood."

Arlene reported another Clint sighting that came on a rainy Monday evening when the actor, who is an accomplished pianist, shared the piano bench with Burt Bales. A legendary San Francisco jazz man, Burt was the walking wreckage of a hard-drinking life. His face was pale and pock-marked like the melted wax accumulating at the base of a white candle. Burned at both ends. His eyes, set deep in hooded eye sockets, had a Jack Elam leer. And, he spoke disjointedly in a growl through barely parted lips. But, the music still ran through him like muscle memory.

The two of them side by side at the piano, the remnants of Burt and Clint, perpetually beautiful, must have been quite a contrast.

Paul Kantner, guitarist and co-founder of Jefferson Airplane (Starship by that time) was a sometime customer, always alone, always uncommunicative, and always ordered the same thing: fried calamari. He was never comfortable enough to say "I'll have my usual" even though I wrote down his order before he spoke.

Personally, I never developed a taste for calamari, which I viewed as a hybrid of bath mats and rubber bands. But, WSB&G's fried calamari, with a dip of anchovy mayonnaise, was very popular and the orders went like this:

"How's the calamari tonight?"
"Excellent."
"Really?"
"Yes."
"Nice and tender?"
"Oh, yes, it's milk fed."
"Okay, I'll have that."

Sports' figures, though not as recognizable as other celebs, were also regulars. Jim Schmitz, who owned the Sports Palace, a gym specializing in weightlifting and competition training, had also been an Olympics coach. He would bring in his beefy crew prior to big contests for carbo-loading which I facilitated with pasta suggestions and outrageous dessert combinations. The Sports Palace group might include, Bruce Wilhelm, an Olympics competitor in weightlifting and shot put, and World's Strongest Man title holder in 1977 and '78.

Needless to say, Bruce was a giant of a man—with a personality to match. He once tossed me over his shoulder and carried me around the dining room.

One of my favorite people from the sports' world was Barry Tompkins, the on-camera commentator, best known for his boxing coverage and appearances as himself in *Rocky* films. He was so lively and clever, always upbeat and approachable. As he was single, I wondered if flirting with Barry would get me anywhere. My appalling lack of sports' knowledge probably doomed that.

What I knew about baseball was based on the Yogi Berra formula. Yogi was thought to be a bit dim, so an interviewer asked how he processed the complexity of the game. Yogi said, "When they throw it, I hit it. When they hit it, I catch it."

So, when Brian St. Pierre asked me to watch a baseball game with him, I prepared for the usual boredom. However, Brian explained the intricacies of the game in a mesmerizing way. I was so enthusiastic, I said "That was great! When can we watch another game?"

Brian laughed and replied, "Not until next year. That was the final game of the World Series."

Luckily for him, Barry escaped my wiles and married the perfect person, sports' writer, Joan Ryan.

Sports' figures comprised just a slice of the celebrities, who turned up at WSB&G. And, the atmosphere usually seemed to put all of them at ease. Robin Williams lived in Marin County and dined occasionally at WSB&G always with a group of friends. At that point in his career, he was known locally for his genius standup and improv performances, enjoyed wider exposure in the TV show *Mork and Mindy,* and was fast-tracking to the Big Time.

Nevertheless, he made me think of the phrase "alone in a crowd." While his companions engaged in revelry, Williams, who was kind and polite in demeanor, generally was the quiet center of the gatherings, only rousing himself, now and then, to prime the pump of merriment with a jocular quip.

Actor Brian Dennehy had a prolific career in stage, film, and television where he played good guys and obnoxious bad guys. The latter probably didn't require as much acting.

John Heard and three other actors, including Rip Torn, arrived one evening. Heard was insufferable, impolite, and hindering the delivery of anything drinkable or edible for the others. Finally, Rip Torn, said apologetically, "Don't mind him. He's in character."

I wondered "In character for what, a brat that's going to bed without supper?"

Ed Moose relished the celebrity clientele and could be over-the-top in schmoozing them. He spotted Lillian Hellman sitting in a window table and oozed in her direction. Hellman's bio put her a cut above contemporary celebrities, not only for her numerous successful plays and screenwriting creds, and her longtime relationship with writer Daishell Hammet, but because she refused to testify when called before the House UnAmerican Activities Committee.

Smoking in restaurants was still allowed in those days and Hellman was smoking a cigarette. Rubbing his hands together, Ed leaned toward the grande dame and said "Ms. Hellman, I apologize. It's so noisy and smoky in here today."

Hellman's wrinkled, tanned face looked like an alligator handbag. Expelling a fog of her own cigarette smoke, she croaked "I like noisy, smoky bars."

On any given evening, the effervescence of the dinner hour might be invaded by what seemed to be an ambulatory pile of rags—Millie the Flower Lady. A tiny, toothless, old person, wearing a cape and a shapeless cap over a cheap wig, Millie modeled her "business" on the leggy cigarette girls that were once a feature of fancy night clubs. A tray of wilted flowers was suspended by a strap around her neck and a greasy Polaroid camera dangled from somewhere. Stuck through all that was a walking cane, which protruded at just the right height to whack a food server across the knees or goose a backside.

Millie would approach tables, extend a drooping flower to a gentleman (which rumor said she collected from the graves at Colma cemetery) and say "Hey, Mifter, wanna buy a fwower for the wady?"

The house policy and the inclination of the staff was to accommodate Millie's capitalist spirit at the same time mollifying startled customers that they were actually lucky to be glimpsing a real-life San Francisco character like they'd heard about, the rarest of all subspecies—North Beach fauna.

In fact, Millie was something of a celebrity in the City as it was in those days. *All characters great and small, San Francisco loved them all.* When Polaroid announced the discontinuation of its instant cameras, Millie fans bought up all available film so she could continue taking pictures. Apparently, Millie never degreased the lens, so her photos had the soft-focus effect long before fashion photographers discovered the technique.

[After being a North Beach fixture for decades, Millie passed in 2017 at the age of 94. She was not forgotten, countless people expressed love for her, and unearthed their own Millie Polaroids, which they had treasured for years.]

Sam Deitsch was unflustered by celebrities. In fact, Sam had adopted unflustered as a lifestyle. I witnessed an incident where Sam was seated at a small table talking to a friend when a malcontent came into the bar, purchased a carafe of red wine from the bartender, Cyril Boyce, walked to Sam's table, and slowly poured the contents over Sam's head.

With remarkable aplomb, Sam sat under the stream drumming his fingers on the table until the carafe was empty. Then, he stood up, mopped his shirt with a napkin, and called out to Cyril, "Please 86 this guy."

Celebrities, in a minor key, were part of Sam's family. He seemed proud of Fran's accomplishments as a song writer, and also seemed to admire the Landesman clan that Fran married into. Sam said "Jay Landesman has the most avant garde taste of anyone I know. Always ten years ahead. Important people hang out with him to find out what's about to happen…"

That seemed to be an accurate description of Fran and Jay's sojourn in St. Louis. But, Gaslight Square was damaged by a tornado and the neighborhood was declining into criminality and worse yet, cheesy, hipster imitators. Time for the cool people to get out.

By 1964, Sam was ready for something different. He sold his share in the Golden Eagle bar and joined the Mooses in San Francisco. That same year, Fran and Jay, along with sons, Cosmo and Miles Davis, moved to London, where they believed they could recapture their avante garde St. Louis success in what was to become the heyday of the Swinging Sixties.

Describing the London sojourn, Sam described Jay as "... [A] publisher who runs a salon. Their regular house guests have included the Beatles, Lenny Bruce, Kenneth Tynan, and Jonathan Winters."

That sounds rather grand and genteel and may have been reported to Sam with sanitized editing. The facts seem otherwise. The couple, who had embraced the Beatnik/bohemian vibe of Gaslight Square, launched themselves fully into the Hippie atmosphere of London with wild parties, long hair, beads, age-inappropriate clothing, their widely discussed open marriage, and serial attempts to Be Somebody—again.

A London contemporary described them as "...[T]wo wacky, middle-aged American egotists who arrived in 'the land of the stiff upper lip' and caused mayhem. Blind to their own blush-making toxicity, they were obsessed with being famous."

That mayhem and toxicity fell heavily on their son, Cosmo, who became a successful journalist, but recorded his tumultuous childhood and the stresses of his parents' flagrant love affairs in his memoir, *Starstruck: Fame, Failure, My Family and Me.* He records the humiliation and pain of the serial assignations which were openly acknowledged, even celebrated, by Fran and Jay, at the same time he preserved affection for his oddball parents.

His parents constantly cooked up projects in the form of books, plays, performances, poetry readings, and potential TV appearances, that would get them back in the spotlight and were endlessly foisted on publicists, movie makers, producers, nightclub owners, and famous friends. Cosmo reported Fran's search for a new agent this way:

Agent: I'm a lousy agent, but a terrific lover.
Fran: Too bad. I have a lousy lover, what I need is a ter-
rific agent.

Apparently, Fran and Sam shared the same biting wit.

On two occasions, I overheard Sam and Ed speaking in serious tones about someone named Cosmo. At that time, I merely thought "Interesting name, Probably not De' Medici."

Was Sam aware of the painful adolescence of his nephew, who was shunted aside while his parents pursued the spotlight? Who regularly woke up to a succession of his parents' new lovers at the breakfast table? Whose own burgeoning success as a writer was fodder and fair game for Fran and Jay's insatiable appetite of another shot at fame?

Was there anything Sam could have done? Cosmo told me Sam had not been a part of his life in London, but was very generous to him when he visited San Francisco. Suzy O'Neill, a longtime friend of Sam's, recalls meeting Cosmo on that visit. Sam liked to cook and entertain, said Suzy. And, his custom was to spread newspapers on the bed and serve dinner there. She wondered what his nephew thought of the dining arrangements. But, those little quirks probably didn't even raise a blip on Cosmo's Family Bizarro Meter.

Family matters were not something Sam and I discussed. He once told me that he was "relieved" when his parents had passed away. Relieved of what? Expectations? Obligations? The clunky baggage each of us hauls out of childhood? Nor did he offer any telling specifics about his relationship with Fran.

So, the particulars of his sister's life were revealed to me by obituaries that provided details when Fran and Jay both passed away in 2011. And, I read Cosmo's book, *Starstruck,* where once again a sense of humor was a survival tool. So, it's only in retrospect that I wonder how Fran and Jay's grotesque behavior and heedless parenting contributed to Sam's prickly personality, his aversion to marriage, and his clarity about the dark side of celebrity.

4

Artists & Artsy Spots

The delights of the beloved North Beach neighborhood radiated in every direction from its spiritual center, the church of Sts. Peter and Paul. The Catholic church with its Romanesque Revival architecture and towering twin spires arose from the neighborhood like an opulent wedding cake. It was fronted by the greensward and shade trees of Washington Square Park.

Overlooking the petite park was Mario's Bohemian Cigar Store Café (Mario's to the locals) the place, in pre-Red Bull days, to boost your energy with a tiny cup of espresso. The view was even better when Mario's handsome son, Paul, was manning the espresso machine.

Nearby was Gino and Carlo, a saloon for those who took their drinking seriously. Capp's Corner, Caffe Sport, Lorenzo's North Beach Restaurant offered red sauce, Sicilian, and Tuscan fare. At the intersection of Columbus and Broadway, a big sign for the Condor Club proclaimed Carol Doda's most famous assets. Nearby

Finocchio's presented drag shows. Beach Blanket Babylon at Club Fugazi, which gave campy presentations with opulent costumes and hat tricks, was a tourist favorite.

One block away, was Vesuvio Café, famous as a Beatnik hangout, which gleamed with multi-colored paint and whimsical images. Next door was Lawrence Ferlinghetti's City Lights Bookstore and Publishing, a gathering place for artists, writers, and activists in the Beat heyday.

Across the street, was Specs' 12 Adler Place. The owner of the knick-knack crammed saloon was Specs Simmons, a colorful, puckish dispenser of wit and wisdom, who mockingly called his bar "my toilet". He wore thick glasses, sported a goatee, and had growly voice so deep that writer Carl Nolte said "…[S]ounded like a load of gravel falling off a truck."

His saloon reflected his sensibilities. Established in 1968 as a hangout for the working-class and trade unionists, 12 Adler Place was popular with artists, writers, merchant seamen, colorful regulars, and celebs, who appreciated its poetry readings and pop-up shenanigans. A big wheel of cheese with saltine crackers was the menu.

Specs also had a penchant for travel. Acknowledging the bartender reputation for skimming cash from the till, Specs, whether headed out the door for an evening of drinking and socializing in the neighborhood, or a fishing trip on the Delta, or an extended stay at the San Juan Islands, would toss the keys to the bartenders and say "Just leave me enough to live on, guys."

He knew something about living on, having survived a near death experience, to which he gave his trademark flippancy. In 1969, Specs and four other bartenders made a boozy, late night decision to take a boat trip to Los Angeles. The craft foundered outside the Golden Gate and sank leaving the five men clinging to four life vests and signaling with a flashlight as an outgoing tide was carrying them towards the Farallons.

Miraculously, the owner and crew of the yacht *Santana*, which had been owned by Humphrey Bogart, saw the feeble signal and hauled the men from the freezing water. A hypothermic Specs was offered a brandy to which he impishly replied "What are you pouring?"

Specs and I went on a day trip to the Delta to fish from the river banks and levees. The temps became so blistering hot, we were going to fry or die. So, we packed up the gear and took refuge at Foster's Bighorn in Rio Vista, a hidden treasure from a by-gone era. The funky dive bar was packed with taxidermy mounts of all sizes. We sat at the bar drinking gin and tonics under a massive African elephant whose trunk extended over our heads.

We clinked glasses and noted that we were safely within British propriety in matters of boozing, that being, gin and tonic should only be consumed in the tropics.

Close to Spec's was the Tosca Café where a huge, antique, cappuccino machine, looking like a silver fireplug, sat on the bar and opera was on the sound track. Hearing opera in North Beach was common. Old Italian men playing bocce ball in Washington Square Park, might pause from their games to belt out Puccini or Verdi.

The neighborhood was almost a world unto itself in those days. So much so, that Sam rarely crossed its boundaries. Like Sam, waitress Sofi Kurtz was a New Yorker and Jewish, which gave the two of them a special connection of culture, background, Big Apple touchstones, and humor. Ever a cheeky provocateur, Sam used to say "When other Jews complain to me about anti-Semitism, I tell them 'So, don't be so Semitic'."

Sofi had to confront Sam about being North Beach bound. She wanted to treat him to dinner at Chez Michel on Northpoint and Hyde at the fringes of Russian Hill. Sam was in a dither that suggested an assault on Everest summit was in the offing. Finally, Sofi said "Sam, if you're so worried, bring your passport!"

In the other direction, where Columbus Avenue headed away from the Beat and Bohemian attractions, was the San Francisco Art Institute and close at hand, one of my favorite places, the Charles Campbell Gallery. The unassuming building regularly featured California artists whose work and new directions I admired—and hoped to emulate.

After nine years bouncing around in colleges, I finally got a degree. At the University of Florida, I majored in British History and minored in Shakespeare. No guidance counselor ever pointed out that, should teaching jobs on those topics appear, they would probably go to graduates of Oxford or Cambridge.

Having all but stamped "Unemployable" on my forehead, I took a break from college to travel, to be a ski bum in Killington, Vermont and Aspen, Colorado, to briefly attend NY Institute of Photography in NYC, and tried my hand at freelance photography in Boston.

When I returned to college at Florida Atlantic University, tuition was cheap, which I could easily finance by waitressing. I could satisfy my interest in theater, art history, and studio art. College administrators finally caught wise after a number of years that I was taking advantage of undergraduate tuition rates, and mailed me a degree, Bachelor of Fine Arts. Given all the tuition I'd paid, it seemed the admins could have included a mortar board to wear while opening the envelope.

Thus, I had some art knowledge when I would visit the Campbell Gallery on Chestnut Street, and I was mesmerized by the offerings: Nathan Olivera, Richard Diebenkorn, James Weeks, Elmer Bischoff, Gordon Cook, and Wayne Thiebaud.

Beyond greetings, I didn't speak much to Charles, who seemed rather reserved, but he certainly recognized me because of my frequent appearances. In any case, contemplation of the paintings, not conversation, was the point of my visits. So, I didn't know what to expect from Charles on a particular day.

A man and his young son, who clearly were not artsy types, had somehow found Campbell's gallery where the featured artist was Wayne Thiebaud during the period of his sumptuously impasto paintings of cakes, pies, and ice cream cones. Father and son studied all the paintings, then settled in front of a small canvas depicting a slice of cherry pie.

Dad said "So, is this the one we want?" Youngster nodded enthusiastically. Turning to Charles, the father asked "How much is this one?"

I dreaded that a withering, artsy putdown might follow. Charles said "Six hundred dollars." In response to the father's chagrin, Charles did something endearing. He assumed some of the embarrassment himself, saying "I know. Isn't that amazing? I wish I had bought it years ago."

Wayne Thiebaud gave two lectures at the Art Institute that I attended. In each case, he opened by saying that he was an artist not a speaker, then proceeded to induce laughter and tears and sublime pleasure in the audience. One of the lectures was directed toward art students and the attrition rate that real life imposes upon them. Only one in ten were likely to carry on, he said, but offered that the impulse to make art, which began with cavemen, is a continuum that connects artists throughout the ages. "When I use pastels," he said "I feel that Degas holds me by the wrist."

One of the Campbell Gallery stalwarts, Gordon Cook, lived in the nearby Russian Hill neighborhood with his charming Irish-born wife, Liadain O'Donovan, who was the daughter of Irish writer Frank O'Connor. Gordon turned up occasionally at the Washington Square Bar & Grill. Gordon struck me as a blue collar-artist combination on the order of longshoreman-philosopher, Eric Hoffer. Somehow, I had the notion he was a starving artist. (Unbeknownst to me, Gordon had income as a union typesetter.) But, I wanted to be sure the big, shaggy guy had enough to eat. Once he ordered a carpaccio special. He looked bewildered after finishing a couple thin slices of raw beef sprinkled with a few capers and a couple scrapings of Asiago cheese. I told him there was something we'd like his opinion on and brought him a big bowl of chunky minestrone soup.

Another North Beach *habitué* was artist Sam Provenzano, who I considered a poseur and a nuisance. He frequented neighborhood cafes and took up space at tables where he slouched with a sketchbook supposedly capturing images of the passing parade in scrawled pencil images enhanced with watercolor. I think a beret and cigarette holder may have been part of his cartoonish affectations.

Provenzano had an actual resume, operated several art schools, and had gallery shows. But, his practice of sketching in popular hangouts, then returning to present the owners with the *artwork* matted, framed, wired, and ready to be hung, I felt, was strong arm self-promotion. And, if the display area of the unasked-for art wasn't sufficiently prominent, he let it be known.

The only people I knew, who had Provenzano pegged and would openly eye-roll, were Specs Simmons and Sam Dietsch, both of whom had *irreverent* in their DNA. Ed Moose described Provenzano as a "boulevardier" and a Sicilian Toulouse-Lautrec. Mary Etta Moose, who apparently took water color lessons from Provenzano, said "He was able to loosen his students up enough to let the water do the work" which sounded more like irrigation than art.

Among the real deals, who frequented the WSB&G, was artist Dugald Stermer, known at that particular time for his stunning, unmistakable illustration work. He came from Southern California where he studied graphic arts at UCLA, and migrated to San Francisco in the 1960s to be art director for the Leftist magazine *Ramparts.*

His studio was on the second floor of a building on Union Street where he could be found at his art desk, lined with pencils, brushes, and tiny bottles of Doc Martin's liquid watercolors, all of which he would graciously put aside for an occasional visitor.

I had a crush on Dugald, as did every woman I knew. I once saw him dining with poet and prolific writer, Maya Angelou, and she seemed crush-y, too. Like Sam, Dugald had a daily wardrobe preference. His was a cowboy vibe—western boots, leather vest, jeans, and bib shirts like the cavalry officers wore in old movies.

Owing to the breadth of his talent, charity work, mentoring, and service to the arts' community, Dugald was comfortable with all kinds of people. His wedding to novelist, Jeanie Kortum, reflected that, as well as the couple's quirky sensibilities. The ceremony featured a pig roast and party at the Kortum family farm in Petaluma, with hay bale seating, tin wash tubs overflowing with booze and beer on ice, and live music. As the sun began to set, an antique fire engine delivered the bride to the wedding bower, while a biplane flew overhead towing a banner that read "All the comedies end in marriage," a nod to Shakespeare.

The Washington Square Bar & Grill had an in-house artist, Gary Epting. A native of Traverse City, Michigan, Gary came west with several friends all of whom worked in the restaurant business while pursuing other interests. Gary was tall, with thinning hair, and a long, usually unsmiling face. Despite his somber look, he was hilarious, mischievous, very well-read, and already a skilled artist. We bonded over art history, visits to SF MOMA, gallery openings, and most things British.

One hectic evening, the WSB&G dining room was jammed, and rowdy with the antics of famed quarterback, Terry Bradshaw, who was joking loudly with another famous quarterback (Hornung?) on the opposite side of the room. Other diners were thrilled with the banter. Gary reported that he was waiting on a pleasant British couple, who'd never seen anything like the hilarity, but were fascinated.

I cruised by the Brits' table to check them out and informed Gary he was serving actor Tom Courtenay, who'd just attended the Oscars where he'd been nominated for the 1983 film, *The Dresser*.

Another visiting Brit was Quentin Crisp, an author, actor, wit, homosexual, and cross-dresser, who was flamboyantly out back when it was still taboo. His self-deprecation was wildly funny. When asked about his unconventional life, he said "Other boys wanted to be firemen or police men. I wanted to be a chronic invalid."

In the 1980s, Crisp was wearing his white hair in a towering blue-rinsed pompadour. The skin of his face, pale and blue tinged, sagged in concentric rings, which gave him the look of a freshly shucked oyster. Awestruck by Crisp's unique façade, I asked Gary "What paint would you use for his portrait?" to which Gary, referencing a durable exterior paint brand, said "Sears Weather Beater."

Gary was then painting commissioned portraits, which reflected years of study and practice. My familiarity with art history allowed me to see who some of his influences were and added to my appreciation of his growing skills. He said his aim was to "see an image and commend it to his hand."

A proper art education takes years. First, in learning to see. Then, in commending the image to one's hand. I was nowhere near that advanced in my training. One of my favorite instructors at FAU believed a young artist should study and practice for ten years before attempting to show their work. However, I was drawing fairly well after struggling to achieve competence.

Drawing from life (yes, that's nude models) was required every semester in art college. At one point, I was so inept, the drawing instructor said my figures looked like "balloon animals." That stinging criticism prompted me to up my game. As did *Critique* which happened every Friday.

During that scalding experience, each student presented what they deemed their best work that week, to be appraised by instructors and fellow students. Harsh though it may have been (and often was) good suggestions were made—and temporary humiliation has a way of affixing lessons more effectively than sugar coating.

In this era of participation trophies and coddling self-esteem, I wonder if Critique is still part of art training.

So important is drawing to seeing and commending that it's a lifetime habit for serious artists. Some of the California artists, who exhibited at Charles Campbell's gallery, met regularly to draw at Gordon Cook's studio. I was invited to pose, but didn't. The possibility of being unclothed was less daunting than the presence of so many art icons.

Fortunately for me, the Fort Mason Art Center was mere blocks from my flat in the Marina District. The warehouses on the piers, where once U. S. troops embarked for the Pacific Theater in WWII, had been repurposed as a well-equipped community art facility. I could grab a big newsprint sketch pad, a couple Blaisdell pencils, a kneaded eraser, and take in the regularly scheduled Life Drawing classes where easels and nude models were provided for a couple dollars.

On one occasion, I noticed a familiar San Francisco face among the sketchers—poet, publisher, book store owner, Lawrence Ferlinghetti. While the model took a break to stretch and relax, I sneaked a peek at Ferlinghetti's easel. He was not even close to balloon animals. More like amoebas. No harm in that. Everyone has to start somewhere. But, Degas would not be holding him by the wrist any time soon.

A few weeks later, I happened to be in City Lights Bookstore. To my amazement, I saw the amoebas displayed, not under refrigerator magnets, but on the walls. It's dispiriting to see people who've made their mark in one area—Ferlinghetti in poetry, Jim Carrey in comedy, George W. Bush in politics, and Hunter Biden in decadence—announce they've become artists and jump the line of those, who've spent years learning the craft.

5

Drinking & Getting By

California has always welcomed The Thirsty. In the colonial period, Spanish missions were established one day's ride apart. The padres planted grapes to make sacramental wine and for their own consumption. They could offer travelers wine and fresh horses.

When Gold Rush prospectors, flush with dust or nuggets arrived in the big city, they were looking to drink the best money could buy or rotgut.

Unsuspecting saloon-goers that frequented the San Francisco establishment of James "Shanghai" Kelly, might be kidnapped and forced to work on sailing ships, after drinking one of his opium-laced cocktails.

Even in the 1950s and Sixties when weed, acid, mushrooms, and other drugs provided altered consciousness, drinking still went on enthusiastically. Perhaps, it's that legacy of imbibing taken to the ultimate that made San Francisco in the 1980s a drinking town, a sloshing, swashbuckling, liver-challenging, town.

The neighborhoods of San Francisco, flavored by the immigrants who settled there, gave preference to the spirits of their native lands.

The Mission district bars might stock a greater variety of tequilas for Latino customers. The Sunset district, location of the Irish Cultural Center, might drink more Guinness and Bushmills than elsewhere in the city. The inner Richmond, around the Russian Tea Room, was geared to a taste for vodka. Saki in Japantown. Baijiu in Chinatown. But, the bountiful booziness that gushed forth in North Beach made it the alcohol Spindletop of San Francisco.

In addition to the wines of Italy, those with esteemed labels and those poured from humble jugs at dive bars, there was a range Italian spirits and cocktails that took a bit of getting used to for newcomers to North Beach. Campari, a bitters' distillation, ruby red in color, was the quintessence of the Negroni and Americano cocktails. Grappa. Galliano. Amaretto. The infamous CBA, hot coffee with brandy and anisette. Sambuca with a coffee bean in footed cordial glass after dinner. And then, there was Fernet Branca, the most potent of the Italian digestifs. Fernet always made me think of Jerry Lewis.

When I was in the college of art at Florida Atlantic University, I worked at Abbey Road steakhouse and lounge in Boca Raton. Mouthwatering steaks and prime rib, cut in house, plus live entertainment nightly, made it a popular destination. Other than local personalities, though, we didn't get celebrities. So, it was a big deal that legendary comedian Jerry Lewis would be dining at Abbey Road.

Yeah, big deal. The first waitress, who attempted to take a cocktail order for Lewis and his party, collapsed in tears at Lewis's rudeness. Abbey Road co-owner, Chuck Faremouth, sent me in. Thirst had prevailed, Lewis's crew was ready to drink, and the comic switched from abuse to wisecracks. One of the guests ordered bourbon on the rocks. Jerry Lewis quipped "Anyone who would drink bourbon, would eat their own young."

Not a fan of bourbon, I emitted a huge guffaw, which broke the ice with the obnoxious funny man. I was able to take the order, deliver the cocktails, then a round of refills, with no further problems.

A Lewis sycophant took me aside to ask if I'd like the comedian's autograph. I laid it on thick, saying Jerry was a comic genius, *The Nutty Professor* the funniest movie I ever saw, and I wouldn't think of imposing on his valuable time for an autograph. Apparently that baloney-laden blandishment was conveyed to Lewis because he was happy and expansive from then on. Lesson learned: Even legends need high fives.

I often wondered what the so-called "King of Comedy" would say about Fernet Branca, and the potential for eating one's own young. The bitterest of bitter extracts, Fernet was supposedly the ultimate digestif for settling a bad tummy and choked down by women for quelling menstrual cramps. Classic dilemma of cure worse than the cause. I described the flavor of Fernet as the taste of sweat from Satan's armpits. Nevertheless, Fernet was consumed in great quantities by North Beach old-timers. A few years back, the makers of Fernet announced a number of new cocktails based on their product. Now that would be interesting.

Sidebar: Pisco is a Chilean/Peruvian brandy, definitely not Italian. Brian St. Pierre and I were bellied up to the bar at a Spanish tapas restaurant. A customer took a seat and signaled his order to the bartender saying "Pisco sour." Brian turned to me and said "That's true. I used to have a cat."

In addition to local Italian drinks, bartenders at Washington Square Bar & Grill, of course, prepared American classics, Old Fashioned, Manhattan, Rob Roy, Tom Collins, Whiskey Sour. Since it was the era of the three-martini lunch, the bartenders dispensed variations on the theme: gin or vodka, up or down, olive or twist. I had not developed a taste for gin or martinis, a sin of omission that Hal Thunes, in the role of priest/bartender, sought to cast out.

He seated me at the bar and assembled the instruments for my conversion like a cleric preparing to serve mass. He set out the glass portion of a cocktail shaker, a long handled stirring spoon, a strainer scrupulously cleansed of any foreign pollutants, a chilled stemware glass, and the ingredients, dry vermouth and Bombay London Dry Gin (no need in those days to say "original".)

On the label, Hal pointed out the botanicals that made Bombay his favorite: angelica root, almonds, cassia bark, licorice, coriander, lemon peel, orris root, and juniper berries. The ingredients, as Hal presented them, made Bombay gin sound like a health drink. Special attention was given to the juniper berries which he claimed had hallucinogenic properties. Mention was made of birds flying loop-de-loops after consuming fermented juniper berries.

Into the ice-filled glass shaker, with a flick of the wrist, went a splash of dry vermouth. Then Hal gently poured in the Bombay and stirred reverentially. When the martini was strained into the stem glass, the liquid assumed an opalescent sheen. The sacrament was almost complete.

Hal suspended a lemon peel over the surface and told me to watch closely. With a twist, the peel expelled a shower of golden droplets that floated on the surface of the gin. The bruised peel was circled around the rim of the glass to further tickle the nose with citrus fragrance. Hal added two green olives skewered with a frilled toothpick. Olive and twist might offend purists, but Hal always knew what the ladies liked.

The drinking that went on at WSB&G was prodigious, starting with the partners. Sam and Ed tended their business every day, arriving in late morning looking fresh and frisky, and jump-starting their amiability with coffee and brandy or the more powerful variant, the CBA. Each of them adhered to a routine of increasingly potent cocktails during the day. They both took breaks at midday when they went home, presumably to nap and dry out. Then, they returned to consume heavier stuff during the dinner hour and close out the night with brandy or cognac.

As a seasoned observer of the pickling process among regular customers, I could usually pinpoint the moment when a drinker tipped from functioning fun-seeker to overserved, but somehow, still functioning boozer, by a look traditionally termed "pie-eyed."

Sam and Ed were often pie-eyed by late evening, but that was the only blotto indicator. They could continue to converse humorously, manage the business affairs competently, and walk out the door at the end of the evening more or less the way they entered in the morning. And, repeat the same process day after day.

The same was true for many high-profile devotees of WSB&G, particularly writers. San Francisco has a history of hard-drinking writers and newspapermen, which was carried on in the 1980s. The *Chronicle* and *Examiner* newspapers had dive bars close to their front doors, so the journalists could readily sluice the Muse. When deadlines were met, the print celebs travelled across town to WSB&G.

Curmudgeonly *Chronicle* columnist Charles McCabe dropped in occasionally, but preferred the grittier atmosphere and the Rainier Ale available at Gino and Carlo. Nicknamed the "Green Death," Rainier Ale got mixed reviews, some of which are hilarious: "…nasty smell, nasty taste, leaves a little suede jacket on the tongue…ah, damn, this is harsh stuff…produces obnoxious farts…"

While McCabe's palate was attuned to Green Death, Ed Moose was not to his taste. McCabe supposedly registered his assessment of Ed as "A fellow who's always looking over your shoulder to see if someone more important has arrived."

Ron Fimrite had moved on from *Chronicle* sports' columnist to become a senior writer for *Sports Illustrated,* and author of numerous books. Fimrite was released from his *SI* obligation to live in New York when his boss figured Fimrite was famous enough to cover baseball from home base in his beloved San Francisco. Fimrite was part of Ed Moose's inner circle of men friends, who enjoyed good stories, good booze, and a club-iness that probably originates for males in a backyard tree house with a crudely lettered sign "No Gurls Aloud." However, Fimrite was also comfortable with women. He was often the only guy at a table full of women, who were kept laughing appreciatively.

Dan Jenkins was a colleague of Fimrite's at *Sports Illustrated.* His journalistic output, for *SI* and *Golf Digest*, and dozens of books (dozens!) was staggering. As was his alcohol intake. Holding forth in a voice, still telltale with his Texas origins, Jenkins could amuse while consuming drinks at ratio of 3:1 with his table mates, who were not slouches. If I were to create a Gilded Liver Award for prodigious drinkers, Jenkins would be Top Five.

Sally Jenkins, Dan's daughter, was a sports writer at the *Chronicle* and *Examiner*, who moved on to the *Washington Post.* Like Dad, Sally could put away quite a few drinks, and like him, became a prodigious and highly-awarded writer.

Upon her father's death, Sally wrote about the valuable advice he passed along "You have to laugh trouble down to a size where you can talk to it."

Stephanie Salter was another *Chron-Ex* writer with a shapely hollow leg. In a memorable column, she made a daring admission that had huge red-faced potential. When Prince Charles wed Lady Diana on July 29, 1981, Stephanie wrote that her dream of marrying Charles had crashed. If she'd gotten that wrong, it would have been humiliating. Instead, the confession brought a collective gasp from countless women of a certain age, who had girlishly fantasized about somehow meeting Prince Charles and becoming princesses.

C. David Burgin was editor of the *Peninsula Times Tribune* when I first noticed him at WSB&G. He always looked long-faced and sad-eyed as thought he'd just attended the funeral of a close friend. Then, he disappeared for a time when he took over the *Orlando Sentinel* in Florida. In 1985, he was hired by the Hearst Newspapers to revive the *Examiner*, and reappeared at WSB&G where he would slouch at the bar in a rumpled suit, looking like a woeful Beagle peering from an unmade bed.

After a full evening of drinking at WSB&G, Burgin might adjourn to Mulhern's on Buchanan Street where we eventually started chatting. Mulhern's, along with The Brazen Head, were my favorite places for a nightcap in my Marina district neighborhood. Women, having a solitary drink or with a group of friends at a popular bar, didn't have to worry in those days about having drugs slipped into their drinks. Bartenders were protective. Stephanie Salter remarked at how solicitous WSB&G bartender, Neil Riofski, was of creating a comfort zone for women.

Of course, women had to assume their own risks of overdrinking—which I had to do. My drinking had been socializing, wild-oats-sowing, until I was in art school at FAU and working at temptation-rich Abbey Road. Staff didn't drink at work, but poured it on afterwards at bars in Florida that stayed open very late. Days off and dining out with friends were bacchanalian; drinks before dinner, wine with, and brutal after-dinner drinks like Stingers and Rusty Nails.

My art school friends were similarly inclined to overdrink, although not budgeted for premium brands. I backed off temporarily when I awoke one morning to find my newly-purchased MG parked in the shrubbery outside my apartment.

In San Francisco, I was again red-lining. Even ferocious hangovers weren't a deterrent. Until they were. One evening, I stopped at Mulhern's after work for a glass of wine. A few people at the bar were drinking Fuzzy Navels and sent one, then another, to me. I knew better than to drink the sweet concoction of orange juice and peach schnapps, but refusal seemed rude. Then, of course, I had to buy a round.

I had been dancing around alcoholism for years. That night I went to the Prom. The price I paid was a horrendous hangover that lasted four days. The ghastly, gag-a-thon prompted a year-long regimen of Perrier, Calistoga, and club soda with lime. Period. No booze. No wine. That body cleanse was helpful, but, after drying out, the old temptations were still around.

History has many characters, who suggest alcoholism is linked with creativity. Renaissance artist, Carravagio, was a drunk and a brawler. Algonquin Round Table star, writer Dorothy Parker, was an alcoholic. Parisian artists and writers imbibed absinthe aka the Green Fairy, a hallucination-inducing spirit so potent, it was eventually banned in several countries. Edgar Allan Poe, drank heavily until he croaked. Nevermore.

Is the alcohol and creativity connection valid? Anecdotal evidence suggests yes. But anecdotes about abstemious artists aren't as interesting. French novelist, Gustave Flaubert, said, "Be regular and orderly in your life, so that you may be violent and original in your work."

That never really caught on.

My drinking was reserved for after hours and weekends. I didn't drink during working hours. The job was too demanding for mental fuzziness. And, I believed customers deserved my best efforts. One particularly hectic evening, I was trying to accommodate a customer's request. I relayed the situation to Hal Thunes, the maître d' of WSB&G.

With an aristocratic bearing and silver beard, Hal prefigured the "Most Interesting Man in the World," the TV pitchman for Dos Equis beer. He always wore a fresh carnation in his lapel, which he would bestow at the end of the evening on some woman, who would melt into girlish goo. Hal never lost his debonair Cool while orchestrating the nightly madness of seating diners with reservations, trying to find tables for walk ins, welcoming gawkers and bar patrons, while keeping fire lanes open for the staff to work.

When I related the problematic customer request to Hal, he listened calmly, his blue eyes staring at me over his half frame reading glasses, and said, "Judy, sometimes the only correct answer is No."

That bit of advice has served me well over the years. By nature, women may be pleasers, approval seekers, and caretakers. Saying No, as a legitimate position, often came in handy. No discussion, no justification, just No.

In the Eighties, the answer to almost everything was Yes. But, even in those freewheeling days, there was an ominous saying making the rounds. Hal, who was *laissez faire* personified, repeated the sentiment, which was, "I loved San Francisco when I first came here because everything was tolerated. Now I'm starting to hate it for the same reason."

Is that what happened to the City I loved? Did San Francisco lose the ability to say No? Was everything tolerated until the City became intolerable?

Like so many WSB&G employees, Hal was overqualified, certainly in the charm and charisma departments. He could have been doing Something More and doing that well. He was a Los Angeles transplant, who admitted to spotty college education, but chose to parry further exploration of his back story with his signature, straight-faced silliness. He told a would-be biographer that he had once been a "jujube salesman."

He said "People tell me I should get ahead. I'm content to just get by."

Getting by in North Beach wasn't a bad deal for Hal. He knew the sidewalks so well, he could walk, smoke, and read a book at the same time. A paperback novel was always tucked into the back pocket of his trousers, usually a convoluted mystery by Raymond Chandler or Ross Macdonald. Hal was known and loved wherever he went. His drinking binges were forgiven because everyone understood or shared the demons that prompted them. And, knew that eventually drink becomes the demon. So, he was at home in a special neighborhood where getting by was a fine pastime.

Hal and I liked to play Scrabble. I may have had a slightly better vocabulary, but he was ever mindful of the double and triple value squares that would boost his score ahead of mine. One Fourth of July, we bought tickets on a Bay ferry for a water view of the fireworks. We brought the travel Scrabble that had pegs on the tiles and secured our seats on the top deck which was crowded. The ferry cruised leisurely and we awaited darkness.

Then, the fog rolled in through the Golden Gate, thick and cool. The sensible folks below deck where warm and consuming drinks, whereas, we chilly topsiders could only see pastel splotches of fireworks detonating above the fog. Hal set up the Scrabble board and we began to play. Soon, teams formed behind each of us, coaching and pointing out possible word combos. That night my team was better and I finally won. Nowadays, everyone would have been on their phones.

Liam Clancy, an immigrant from Ireland, was a good friend of Hal's. He was a wonderfully funny, frowsy leprechaun and, like Hal, he was content to get by. The two of them once concocted a scheme to go to Hollywood to become actors. Liam, who could talk the ears off a rabbit, managed to get an interview with a female talent agent.

Since, she was taking notes, Liam imagined that she was bewitched by his blarney. When the agent excused herself momentarily, Liam slipped behind her desk to read her notes, which said "Red-faced Irishman. Can't ride a horse."

Menial jobs were enough for Liam. He reserved his brilliance for friends and was content to be a *swamper*, bar talk for a maintenance/odd job/janitor, who mops floors, makes minor repairs, and checks beer kegs. At one time, he was a swamper at "The Committee," the famous improvisation group on Broadway. Founded in 1963 by associates of Second City, the counterculture satirists and performers wore the requisite gear of the Sixties, tie dye shirts, beads, bell bottoms, and sandals. Liam, for the only time in his life, wore a shirt and tie. His reason: "I don't like uniforms."

When Hal and I planned a trip to London, Liam said he would join us after stopping for a week in Ireland for a long overdue family visit. A last-minute situation arose to delay our arrival in London and we needed to advise Liam. But, it hadn't occurred to us, in the days before cell phones and social media, to share contact information. We knew Liam was from the small town of Youghal, which is near Cork, and that his father owned a pub, so we started with Cork. Amazingly, an actual operator in Cork answered the phone. We explained what little we knew, and the operator said "Sure and you must mean young Liam Clancy whose been gone to America these many years and has now come home."

One phone call and done. Apparently, Ireland, like the bar in the TV show, *Cheers*, is a place where everybody knows your name. And, Ireland kept track of its sons and daughters.

Neil Riofski was a hug in human form. His warm brown eyes, under a swag of tawny hair, radiated merriment. His ear-to-ear toothy grin advertised his encompassing hospitality. Barstools on his end of the bar were coveted by patrons, who wished to talk sports, horse racing, wagering, writing, music, and matters of interest to all kinds of people, each of whom felt, for those moments Neil's face shone upon them, that they were the only person in the room.

The *ski* in Neil's name signified Polish heritage in some measure. I never heard him reference John Sobieski III, or even perogies, but he was gently ribbed about his ancestry. Hyphenated Americans were not in effect yet and amusing ethnic jokes in those days were not deemed offensive. On a November day, one of his staunchest admirers came in, but took a seat at the far end of the bar. Neil called out to him "Hey, what ya doing down there?"

The customer called back "It's Election Day. No drinking within ten feet of the Poles."

Partnering Neil on the other end of the bar was Tom Slater, who was Neil's opposite in very way. He was a tall man with black hair and a handsome face that chose to glower. His inquiry about one's drink order was wrapped in a rumble. His menacing demeanor belied a keen sense of humor that occasionally burst out in a formidable roar of laughter. The yin and yang of Tom and Neil tending the plank worked well, and the two were buddies. When the first *Star Wars* movie premiered in 1980, Neil coined a perfect nickname for Tom: Darth Slater.

Writers, who attempted to capture the essence of the Washington Square Bar & Grill, often evoked the name of Damon Runyon, an American newspaperman, whose short stories celebrated an imaginary New York world of gamblers, grifters, and race track regulars, with colorful names. Runyon said, "The race may not always be to the swift or the victory to the strong, but that's how you bet."

Neil, who loved to play the ponies, had a different betting system. He told me "Bet on the grey. If there's no grey, bet the sheepskin noseband."

In 1984, a big black Thoroughbred had won the Kentucky Derby and the Belmont, and was favored to be a Triple Crown winner, but died unexpectedly prior to the Preakness. Neil, who never missed work, was absent one day. In response to customers questioning Neil's whereabouts, Tom Slater joked "He went to Swale's funeral."

Two short stories by Damon Runyon inspired the 1950s musical, "Guys and Dolls," which won a Tony Award for music and lyrics by Frank Loesser. Knowing the lyrics to Broadway musicals was part of being a well-rounded person in those days, and my restaurant colleagues and our customers, sufficiently lubricated, could probably belt out *Luck be a Lady, Oldest Established (Permanent Floating Crap Game)*, and *Fugue for Tinhorns*.

Feminism was in the I-can-open-the-door-myself stage, but how many San Francisco women listened wistfully to *I'll Know (When My Love Comes Along)*—especially when there were so many Sky Masterson types around?

Familiarity with all kinds of music was part of Neil's vast knowledge. Jazz pianist Dick Fregulia, who played the WSB&G upright on Thursday nights, was a rather cerebral, sensitive guy. One evening, mostly for his own enjoyment, Fregulia put together a set of Frank Sinatra tunes from 1953-1961 when the singer recorded with Capitol Records.

To Fregulia's astonishment, Neil, while serving drinks behind the bar, enthusiastically called out not only the song titles, but the albums from which the tunes came, and in what year.

Neil was equally conversant in English Lit. He had a degree from University of San Francisco. I had lots of English Lit in my college background, so we had common ground. We loved the English language and the nuance of its vocabulary. In conversation, we played a game of one-upping each other with arcane word use. *I'll see your reprehensible and raise you an ignominious.*

We once had a disagreement over the correct pronunciation of the word "ululate." Cell phones, internet searches, and the ability to settle bets with a few keystrokes, were years in the future. After consulting hard cover dictionaries overnight, we learned we were both right. If only all disputes worked out so perfectly!

My admiration for Neil went well beyond our playful banter and verbal sparring. I thought of him as a fully formed human being. He had acquired prodigious knowledge, but he wore it so sweetly, so reassuringly that no one felt intimidated or diminished by his mind. His boundless humor, an attribute which is rarely partnered with great intellect, flowed into every part of the staff's activities and enhanced the lives of his multitude of friends.

But, for all the good cheer and camaraderie that Neil generated, he was a tortured soul. At the University of San Francisco, he had been a stand out student, who wrote so brilliantly, there was no doubt he would be the next Hemingway or Norman Mailer or more likely, someone totally unique. However, a painful divorce from a disabled woman, who managed to grind away at his kindness and generosity, left him crippled with guilt and gutted his ambition.

The remorse that gnawed away at him was assuaged with alcohol, more and more as the years went by. Legions of friends watched in despair, begged him to write, to grasp the brass ring of his destiny, to stay and grow old with us. But, he couldn't.

Stuart Sharf had the highest sex appeal of any of the WSB&G bartenders. He was tall, well-built, handsome, and exuded the best kind of testosterone. But, Stu's sterling qualities were humility and endless patience for everyone. He was a bit hard of hearing and would lean in to listen earnestly to whatever tales were being related to him. He dated a series of stunning blonde women. But, he would attend to every woman at WSB&G, from creaky, querulous Lucy Kendall to raven-haired beauty, Debbie Lawder Sullivan, with the same tender solicitude.

We all adored him and saw an opportunity to show it. Stu's preference for blondes was an ongoing source of teasing. As his birthday approached, we secretly planned an all-woman party in the backroom of Mulhern's where each of us would wear a blonde wig. Jo Marie Smith, who was a great friend of Stu's but not affiliated with WSB&G, was our decoy. She lured him to Mulhern's for a supposed lunch date.

When Stu was tricked into the back room, an assemblage of blondes in wacky costumes jumped up to yell "Surprise!" Understandably, he was befuddled at first, probably thought he'd stumbled into a psyche ward, but soon figured out that he recognized the bewigged nut cases who were enveloping him with hugs. The shock had the desired effect. Sometime later, Stu met and became engaged to a beautiful brunette.

Hal had been part of Washington Square Bar & Grill almost from the start. As maître d, standing at the front door with a folded sheet of paper listing reservations, he was the first person that customers saw. The sight of him, handsome and upright, greeting them affably, was an aperitif to an evening likely to have several pleasurable courses.

He was also a father of three, grown or nearly grown, children, two sons and a daughter, all of whom inherited his Nordic good looks. He liked to say "I'm Nor-Wig-Ian. His oldest son Derek was a talented musician and composer whose works were starting to be performed publicly. The Thunes' clan, like North Beach and much of straight San Francisco, were only vaguely aware of a plague gathering in the City's gay enclaves. In 1983, word of "gay cancer" began spreading and the disease was claiming victims quickly after the onset of symptoms. A number of WSB&G staffers were gay. As with race, religion, and national origin, no one cared about sexual orientation if one could fit into the spirit of the place.

Although Washington Square Bar & Grill was not a favored hangout for gays, writer Armistead Maupin with an entourage of young gay men called Army's Army, would stop by occasionally. Maupin's book *Tales of the City* was serialized in the *Chronicle* newspaper. The characters lived on fictional Barbary Lane (based on Macondray Lane) on Russian Hill, which was close enough for the fictitious folks of *Tales* to do fictitious lunch at WSB&G. In the non-fiction world of the HIV-AIDS menace, not much was said in-house to our gay colleagues other than concerns expressed as "Be careful."

Early on, it seemed clear there was a sexual activity component to the relentless disease. Nevertheless, attempts to curtail sexual activity were resisted. Dr. Anthony Fauci has been the front man for AIDS, Ebola, and Covid-19. In concert with other San Francisco health experts, Fauci tried and failed to have the bath houses shut down (although, he successfully shut down and entire country in 2020). Another preventive measure might have been to exclude gay blood donors until the disease was understood.

In that time frame, Derek Thunes was in a serious motorcycle accident. Despite extensive injuries, Derek was expected to live. Then, he was transfused with AIDS-tainted blood and died within days.

6

Family Table Follies

At the back of the main dining room, there was a massive oak table that could be extended and supplemented with leaves to accommodate large parties. From 5-6 pm, the Family Table was where staff gathered for dinner. Our beloved cooks, Manuel and Edgar, endeavored to find time in their busy prep schedule to make delicious meals for us. And, Ernie Cervantes, a tiny, impish, Mexican immigrant, who was the maestro of salads and cold appetizers, would toss together a big bowl of greens and garden vegetables for us.

We all looked forward to that time together. Differences in gender, race, ethnicity, and national origin were of no consequence. The WSB&G crew was diverse before the word *diversity* became a political imperative. Because the diversity grew organically among people with cooperation and common purpose, it succeeded. Mandated diversity and quotas would have worked as well as arranged marriages.

Peter Yeung spoke Chinese-inflected English proficiently. He was a workaholic, holding down two jobs. Slim and sober-faced,

Peter moved with robotic efficiency like an automaton in a tuxedo. Rumors were that Peter worked so relentlessly because his gambling had put him deeply in debt to the wrong people. One day, steadfast Peter didn't show up for work. Efforts to contact him were hampered by the secrecy of Chinatown. We never saw him again.

Two of our other Chinese co-workers, Jimmy and Tim, could not or would not, shed light on Peter's disappearance. Jimmy Chong was the head busboy and another of the unheralded essential workers of WSB&G. In addition to bussing tables and assisting food servers, Jimmy was in charge of linen. The starched white table cloths, chefs' jackets, and aprons, which were stored in a cramped cubby hole, had to be sorted by size, and reordered as needed, tasks Jimmy could perform with his limited language abilities.

Jimmy struggled to make himself understood on more complicated issues. Those of us, who were patient with his attempts and showed our appreciation, were rewarded with invitations to his daughter's lavish wedding reception at a Chinatown restaurant where the proud father was in his element and treated us grandly.

In one of the Dodge Balls that Ed leveled at me, he decreed that I was going to be responsible for managing the linen supplies, an area I knew nothing about and would likely fail. Ham-fisted as usual, Ed didn't anticipate the affront to Jimmy, who took pride in the management of an important responsibility. It's what elevated him above the other busboys. When I tried to learn the ropes, Jimmy expressed, in fractured English, his deep unhappiness at being demoted. So, we agreed that I would occasionally enter the linen closet in Ed's view, and that Jimmy would carry on with the job.

Tim Yee, an immigrant from Hong Kong, graduated from busboy to waiter by improving his language skills. In addition, he adopted the madcap humor that was so much a part of staff interactions. At the Family Table, he would listen intently to the banter and jump in with hilarious quips that cracked us up. He also became a customer favorite.

Coining nicknames became Tim's specialty. One older lady with faded blonde hair, whose normal speaking voice was thunderous, became "Old Yeller." Ernie McCormick, a retired banker, was so laid back, he was called "Ernie McDormant." Stanton Delaplane, who regularly occupied one of Tim's tables for hours each day, was tagged "Stanton Daily Pain." And sharing the staff's collective discomfort with our boss, Tim called Ed "Moosilini."

"Fast Eddie" was a tall, handsome Italian from Milan. His rapid-fire chatter and charm were fueled by cocaine. He claimed that most Milanese were as crazy as he was and offered their driving habits as proof. Heavy fog was common on the roadways of Milan, said Eddie. Drivers, being Italian, weren't about to slow down, so, to see better they drove with their heads stuck out the windows. Most accidents came from cars passing in opposite directions and heads smashing into each other.

Cocaine is virtually synonymous with the 1980s and some staffers were users, though not generally while on duty. One exception was Helmut, who was beloved by all of us for his outrageous, performance art comedy, which was enhanced by blow. He could alternatively appear as Bill Murray, who he resembled, or Robin Williams, or John Belushi.

Helmut asked Sofi to take the dessert order and finish one of his tables. She found the diners completely traumatized. They'd read about WSB&G in travel magazine, like a Triple A restaurant suggestion. They were totally unprepared for Helmut in full John Belushi mode. He had bullied them into ordering the special, which was Rabbit Cacciatore. Then, he returned, threw a carrot onto the table and said "We'll need this to attract the little bugger." In hushed tones, the diners told Sofi "Help us. We're afraid of him."

Fast Eddie was let go. Helmut realized he had a problem and went to rehab in Sonoma.

Bill Oates was a tall black man, who cut an elegant figure in a waiter's tuxedo. He enjoyed Family Table camaraderie and the general hijinks, but didn't tarry for extracurricular activity, probably as a cost-saving measure. He was married to a white woman and the devoted couple enjoyed traveling to sophisticated locales where good dining and comfortable lodgings were available and purchased with money judiciously saved.

Javier was Mexican and resembled Leo Carrillo, the sidekick in the TV show, *Cisco Kid*. However, he wasn't sidekick or team player material. His incessant attempts to corral all the best-tipping customers, to prioritize his orders in the kitchen, and to monopolize the busboys, was not in keeping with the prevailing spirit of cooperation. He was let go. The same was true of a German waiter, whose nickname "Rudy Runamok" says it all.

Arlene Nieman was a waitress, who could sub as a bartender if needed. She was a stunner with ivory skin, a mane of black hair, and Liz Taylor blue eyes. An elderly Italian restauranteur she worked for in the East Bay celebrated her eyes with the nickname "Violetta." She was a transplant from Detroit, who remained a fierce Tigers fan in the midst of Giants' territory. Whenever Tiger coach, Sparky Anderson, visited WSB&G, Arlene greeted him like a favorite uncle.

"Little Tommy" Wilson was a Brit, who was on the top tier of funny guys at WSB&G. Tom was often called upon for the party plans, comedy skits, and stunts, the staff regularly cooked up. One such was a retirement ceremony for Rene and Pierre, two Frenchmen, who were wine reps and salesmen. Rene looked like Charles DeGaulle, in profile and weight, and his associate, Pierre, looked like a Mini Rene.

The Gallic duo had presented numerous wine tastings to acquaint us with the wines they represented, and arranged for a staff picnic at Beringer Vineyards in Napa Valley. They had been so good to us, we couldn't let them return to France without a proper, affectionate, and crazy send off at the Family Table.

I had found a brass plate at an antique store that was meant to identify non-potable water. It read "Unfit to Drink." I added chains and braid and turned it into medal of honor for Rene. On cue, Tom, dressed in drag, was supposed to descend the narrow steps from the upstairs office and present the award to Rene with a kiss.

Tom never did funny by halves. Instead of just donning a wig and a dress, he went deep. After missing his cue a couple times, Tom called down the stairs "My nail polish isn't dry."

Tom, Arlene, and I, also created a Dicken's Christmas Carol spoof. Ed and Sam treated the staff to a holiday get together every year. When the Christmas party was held at Monroe's on Lombard, the three of us gathered at my flat, which was nearby, to get into costumes.

Arlene, as the ominous Ghost of the Future, wore a wraith-like dress, and was slathered in white body paint with spidery white cobwebs wreathed around her hair and shoulders. As the abundant Ghost of the Past, I wore a borrowed tuxedo and a black silk top hat adorned with holly and gold tinsel. Tom was the Ghost of Christmas Present, literally. He had fashioned a box tied with ribbons and a bow, and cut holes for his head, arms, and skinny legs, which were clad in colored panty hose. We couldn't fit Tom in my car, so we walked along Lombard Street to Monroe's much, to the delight of passing motorists, who honked and slowed down for a closer look.

Being amusing at the Family Table was a shared obligation which could be prompted by mundane sources. From handling many credit cards, we learned that some people have hilarious names. Often, it was amazing to think parents had actually saddled a helpless child with crazy monikers. Imagine Mom and Dad, standing at the baptismal font, at the eleventh hour, and still electing to name a boy child "Algonquin Finsterwald."

When we noted a crazy name on a credit card, it was relayed to Gary Epting, who was the collector, and curator of Funny Names. He read the new additions at the Family Table: Bambi Tascarelli, Lucky Pantages, Bonsal Glasscake, Maureen A. Footlick et al.

The intra-squad fun was infectious. We were blessed with customers, who recognized and rewarded the special bond. George Carleton was a well-to-do businessman with a grand home in Burlingame. His wife, Marilyn, was a stunningly handsome woman, and her good looks had been passed on to their children, who were grown. The whole family regularly drove north to the City to dine at WSB&G and the pleasure they had in each other's company was wonderful to see.

George was so pleased at the warm reception they always received, he wanted to return the favor. He gave a pool party with sumptuous food and drink for the entire staff at his home in Burlingame. WSB&G was closed for the day, as no one was expected to be able to function after the Burlingame blow out.

Dugald Stermer arranged a turnabout day, where prominent San Franciscans became waiters and the staff became customers. Dugald, TV reporter Karl Sonkin, and musician Vernon Alley were among the waiters. Writers David Bush and Ron Fimrite tended bar. Thankfully, no one subbed for Manuel and Edgar, or the joint might have burned down.

Sofi's knowledge of sports was so respected and her personality so lively that she was invited to join an all-male Football Club that met weekly for lunch on Thursdays, an amazing coup in the heyday of Good Old Boys. She was so appreciated by prominent sports' attorney, Jeff Walsh, he provided Sofi with tickets to 49ers games.

She also scored tickets from an admirer for *Rigoletto* at the San Francisco Opera and invited me. We got glammed up for the evening. The presentation was in the original Italian. The aria "la donna e mobile" was awesome. The plot was incomprehensible but had something to do with a court jester, a story line I'm always partial to.

At that time, Gary Epting was painting commissioned portraits. Working from photographs and sittings, and using a traditional method of layering washes of oil paint, he achieved luminous images. But, Gary, who had good business sense, saw the potential of tapping into WSB&G's popularity to advance his painting career. He approached select customers and staff offering to paint their portraits.

Now, portrait painters have been rascals throughout art history. While dependent on payment from patrons, they often sneaked in revealing editorial elements about the sitters—to the vague puzzlement of the portrait subject, who was paying the bill. One painter, reflecting a complaint commonly expressed by duped patrons, said "In a portrait, there's something not quite right about the eyes."

Gary was solidly in that tradition. His Family Table mischief was translated onto the canvasses. When Ed found out about the portrait collection, he offered Gary a show on the walls of WSB&G in January 1987. The staff picked up on some of Gary's jests, such as his portrait of Blanche Streeter.

Blanche was a successful realtor at Grubb and Ellis, with a background in newspapers, both hard knock businesses. However, Blanche retained a convivial sweetness, enhanced by a charming sparkle in her eyes. Along with a gaggle of gal pals, who called themselves the "Roses of Washington Square Bar & Grill," Blanche and the Roses, which included lawyer Patsy Glynn, realtors Linda Freeman and Ellen Edmundson, fitness trainer Martha Cason-Majors, and others, took long hard-drinking lunches.

Gary's portrait depicted the moment when the sparkle in Blanche's eyes, flipped to over-served and pie-eyed—a switcheroo that all the waiters recognized. Certainly, a case of something not quite right about the eyes.

Viewers of the show wondered if Gary was employing symbolism, which he denied. I knew better. His depiction of Ed, Sam, and manager Mark Shachern, I recognized as a straight up homage to a Holy Trinity composition by a Renaissance artist. Although Unholy was more likely. Ed surmounts the triangle holding a chalice of wine. Sam sits below Ed, consulting receipts and paperwork (pawn tickets for souls?) Mark sits on the left looking meek and submissive.

One of the canvases showed Godzilla amid a group of regulars. Gary maintained that a person in a Godzilla costume had actually come into WSB&G, ordered a drink, and drank it with a straw through a hole in costume's neck. Nevertheless, there was speculation Godzilla represented Ed Moose. *Examiner* columnist, Rob Morse, thought it signified the Health Inspector.

When I confronted Gary with my belief that he was indeed employing symbolism, he smiled and shrugged. That gesture summed up Gary's opaque nature. While he could elicit all kinds of information from people in conversation or divine even more through observation, he chose to remain a mystery to us.

He asked me to pose for a portrait. I cordially declined. Gary's allegiance to his art superseded our friendship. As it should. Truth, as an artist or writer sees it, should prevail. I respected that, but didn't want a Portrait of Dorian Gray depiction of my faults or my own pie-eyed moments hung in that Rogues Gallery.

Laughter was the adhesive for everything at Washington Square Bar & Grill. Salubrious, inventive, healing, companionable, human comedy, laughter. We all enjoyed being clever and interesting to each other. And, to wrap laughter around our interactions; to close the gaps between us, the inescapable disparities of existence, with warm chuckles.

One of the dreariest, most damaging features of the 2020s is the absence of laughter. The Torquemadas of Political Correctness persecuted humor until it shrank to nothing. They shoveled away the common ground between people and left only tiny islands of homogenized humans shouting at each other "That's not funny!"

The egalitarian atmosphere of the Family Table was reflected in the variety of patrons that frequented WSB&G. Moreover, there seemed to be a fluidity in 1980s San Francisco between class and race that mixed together different groups. Barriers to societal interactions were permeable. The swells, who usually patronized the Tonga Room at the Fairmont and Trader Vic's, were known to rub elbows with saloon denizens.

Such was the case with Terry Black, who was an interior decorator/designer to high society, and a walker for a rich old lady. He was aggressively nasty when drunk and was usually half in the bag by the time he arrived for dinner, generally with a large party. The sight of him moved waiters to prayer (Please, God, not me!) Their prayers were answered but not mine. Black's desire to be highly visible and to be seated in the front station meant I was often stuck with him.

For a number of sessions, it was miserable. He was abusive, rude, and snappish. The situation had to change. He wasn't going to, so I did. I began to treat him with exaggerated courtesy, giving his orders my highest priority, lavishing him with respect in front of his guests, and fussing over him with cartoonish solicitude. Eventually, he melted like the sugar cube in an Irish coffee.

Mr. Black became a squish, the easiest customer to please, and a lavish tipper. He would take his seat, wave his arm grandly, and say "Judy, you know what we need" and let me do my thing. The other waiters would commiserate that, yet again, I was afflicted with Terry Black. I never divulged my dirty secret: I was very fond of him.

Being part of the wine industry was usually a passport to class fluidity. Except, in the case of a blind Mendocino wine maker, who used to drive down from Mendo' to San Francisco with a group of friends for dinner at WSB&G. Yes, blind, yes, drive. Presumably, with co-pilot guidance. Contrary to beliefs about keeping the palate pure, the blind wine maker was a heavy cigarette smoker.

In the early days, smoking was allowed in Washington Square Bar & Grill. Later smoking was banned in the dining room, but permitted on the bar side. Sam, who was a smoker, was an ashtray vigilante. Woe to the waiter who allowed two butts to accumulate. One night, the blind wine maker was filling ashtray after ashtray when his sensitive nose sniffed out the aroma of a cigar.

He insisted the cigar smoker extinguish his tobacco choice. When the staff refused to enforce the double standard, the blind wine maker got out of his chair and, with arms extended, crashed about trying to lay hands on the cigar smoker. He was finally mollified with the offer of a free cognac.

A round of drinks *on the house* was a good way to soothe customers who had to wait a long time for a table. And complimentary after dinner drinks were offered as an apology for difficulties with meal service. Many ruffled feathers were relaxed by the free booze, good faith gestures.

One person who traveled easily up and down San Francisco's class ladder was Scott Beach. He was a man of boundless talents— Renaissance Faire performer, improv actor at The Committee, film actor, singer, announcer, radio host, writer, DJ, narrator, furniture and musical instrument maker, freelancer extraordinaire, and bon vivant. He was as comfortable in a tuxedo acting as a deep-voiced emcee for high society, philanthropic events as he was in a cable knit sweater and his trademark fisherman's cap. Scott represented, in my mind, the rich opportunities the City offered to those who had the wherewithal to reach out to grasp them.

Scott appeared in a number of Hollywood films, notably *American Graffiti, The Right Stuff, Mrs. Doubtfire,* and *Stand By Me.* He may have gotten more movie work if he moved to Los Angeles, but his love for San Francisco wouldn't allow for relocation. He enjoyed the city in all its high and low variety, navigating through the neighborhoods on a BMW motorcycle.

The streets of San Francisco, roller coasting over its seven hills, were demanding for any kind of conveyance. My vehicle was a 1975 MGB convertible, the only new car I ever bought. The four-on-the-floor shift was challenging when stuck on a hill behind a cable car or a Muni bus whose antennae had flopped off the overhead power lines. Herb Caen joked that a San Franciscan could be identified anywhere because they curbed their car wheels even in flat-as-a-pancake cities.

I parked my MG all over the city at all times of the day and night. It was never pilfered for change, broken into, damaged, or the vinyl top cut through to steal any belongings. Apparently, it wouldn't last 15 minutes in today's San Francisco. Reportedly, thievery, broken windows, car jackings, and strong-arm robbery of automobile drivers are now common occurrences in the formerly safe city.

Seeing Scott's motorcycle pull up in front of the Washington Square Bar & Grill lightened the heart. Good conversation and amusing stories were going to follow. We shared a love of Shakespeare. Interest in the Bard may have been dwindling in academia, but the American Conservatory Theater on Geary Street regularly included Shakespeare plays in its repertoire and the Renaissance Faire in Marin County was loaded with Elizabethan era fun.

Scott wanted to spend more time talking Shakespeare than hectic dining at WSB&G afforded. He invited me to come to his home for readings. Scott had recently announced, after many years of marriage and two children, that he was a gay man. The assassination of Harvey Milk, a gay supervisor, motivated Scott to acknowledge his true self. Later Scott's mischievous humor prompted him to say that he wished he'd stayed in the closet and just hired a good decorator.

Since Scott was out, I knew his intentions weren't amorous. And, he knew mine weren't either. So, we could comfortably meet, choose a different play for our readings, and sit across from each other at his kitchen table enacting various parts. The tragedies—*Othello, Hamlet, Macbeth*—were the best showcases for Scott's magnificent voice.

Out, out brief candle
Life's but a walking shadow, a poor player,
That struts and frets its hour upon the stage
And then is heard no more.

But we also read the comedies, including my favorite, *Twelfth Night,* which contains a line that speaks to me. Two of the minor characters are Malvolio, a stick-up-the-butt, by-the-book conniving Puritan. He is the steward in the house of Countess Olivia. Malvolio's nemesis is Olivia's uncle, Sir Toby Belch, a fat, roistering prankster and wit, who spends his time eating and drinking the comestibles in Olivia's house. Despite his excesses, Sir Toby is much loved by Olivia.

Thus, when Malvolio is badgering Sir Toby about his habits, the loveable rascal says:

Dost thou think, because thou art virtuous
There shall be no more cakes and ale?

In the current atmosphere of retro-Puritanism, oppressive virtue-signaling, and cancel culture, when a desire for cakes and ale (the good things in life) is deemed greedy, selfish, and inequitable, it's comforting to recall that Sir Toby vanquishes Malvolio.

Musical talent was another passport for traversing class barriers. After 1960, that included black musicians. Previously, black musicians were restricted by Musicians' Union Local 6 to playing west of Van Ness Avenue where they were in demand in the Fillmore district. Legendary bass player, Vernon Alley, lead a fight to open the union and give blacks access to all performance venues and enhance the city's enjoyment of jazz.

Sam, Ed, and Mary Etta, were well-acquainted with jazz and the musical stalwarts of the San Francisco jazz scene. Thus, the upright piano at WSB&G, situated under an enormous mirror for surveying the audience, was occupied on a nightly basis with longtime beloved jazz pianists like Norma Teagarden, Burt Bales, and the inimitable John Horton Cooper. A younger generation of talented jazz pianists, like Mike Lipskin, Dick Fregulia, and Mike Greensill, filled out the roster.

Cooper and his good friend Vernon Alley, had been around forever, having played in the 1950s and Sixties at the El Matador jazz club on Broadway. They were both such affable and articulate men that, first Vernon, then John, broke the color barrier when they were invited to join the Bohemian Club, the ultimate white guys' association.

Ed Moose described John's wardrobe preferences as "Duke of Windsor mode." The sartorial ex-king was always on the cutting edge of fashion, whereas John's taste was more settled. His tweeds and saddle oxfords suggested a 1930s hipster vibe. I thought he had raided Rudy Vallee's closet and never moved on.

John's familiarity with a keyboard was so great, the claim had been made that he could play piano and simultaneously play a game of chess. At the WSB&G, he interspersed conversation with his many fans and friends with piano riffs that Sam called "noodling." Occasionally, Sam would stride up and down during the noodling, waving his arms and wailing "John, give us a song, just one song."

Trips to London to visit his daughter were part of John's life that he thoroughly enjoyed. If that meant running up his credit card, so be it. He told me "Judy, they can kill you, but they can't eat you."

When John learned I was planning a London trip with friends, he recommended a few mandatories, including the famed jazz club, Ronnie Scott's, where I was to mention his name. I didn't realize the depth of John's resume in the world of jazz, and I was squeamish about asking for special favors via name-dropping. However, when we went to Ronnie Scott's to hear legendary drummer, Louis Bellson, and his band, we could scarcely see him from our table, I relayed to our waiter that John Horton Cooper was sending regards to Ronnie Scott. We were immediately moved to a primo table.

Louis Bellson, I believe, was the wit who reconfigured an old saying about bad times being good for some people, when he said "Saxophone is an ill wind that no one blows good." Dick Partee played alto saxophone at gigs all over San Francisco and loved WSB&G as a musician and a customer.

After service in the Navy during the Korean War, which ended in 1953, Dick was demobilized in San Francisco, a place that suited him so well, he rarely left. A black American, he could soon avail himself of rule changes at Local 6, and play wherever he was wanted, and that added up to most of the city's famous jazz spots.

Dick was a good friend, who loved to needle me about a particular incident I shared with him. In the summer of 1969, I was taking classes at the New York Institute of photography in NYC. My budget was so tight, I lived at the downtown YMCA, and ate once a day. A school friend invited me to an event that was happening upstate. But, car troubles prevented us from attending Woodstock.

To console myself, I dipped into my meager piggy bank to buy a balcony ticket at Madison Square Garden to see James Brown and the Fabulous Flames. Everyone else in the cheap seats was black. Bottles in paper bags were being passed around. One of the opening acts drew wild appreciation from our section. I had no idea who it was and asked the man next to me.

He looked at me in utter amazement and said, in a voice that slid around through an octave, "Whhyyy dass Tyyyrooonnne Daaavis!!"

Dick thought that was hilarious and never let me forget it. He liked to sneak up behind me and yell, "Whhyyy dass Tyyroonne Daaavis!!"

Faith Winthrop's career overlapped with Cooper, Alley, and Partee. By the 1950s, when she arrived in San Francisco, Faith was already an experienced and lauded jazz singer. In Brookline, Massachusetts, where she was born, an 11-year-old Faith sang and took requests on as streetcar that ran from Brookline to Boston. Classical opera training followed. However, hearing the incomparable voice and stylings of Sarah Vaughn changed the focus of her singing. She embarked on the peripatetic life of a jazz singer, going from club dates, gigs, and recording sessions around the country, during which she met and performed with countless music icons.

When I knew Faith, she had stepped back from performing to raise her daughter and give lessons in her beautiful Edwardian home on Stanyan Street in the Cole Valley neighborhood that borders Golden Gate Park. In the music studio was a grand piano. The rear windows overlooked a rock garden that blazed with tulip color in the spring. Elsewhere in the house, canaries, lots and lots of canaries, warbled their own tunes.

Faith told me the canary thing began when she found an antique brass canary cage at an antique store. I teased her that it was fortunate indeed she hadn't found an antique camel saddle.

Bird people, I learned, are special. I'd always had pets, usually dogs, and I missed the companionship. On impulse, I bought a cockatiel at a Chinese pet store, with all the equipment that comes with housing and feeding, what turned out to be, a tiny gray pterodactyl. The creature had not been hand-raised as advertised, but viewed hands as a source of fresh blood.

Certain times of day were for ear-shattering screeches and the rest of its waking hours for spewing seeds, shells, and poop outside its cage, which earned its name "Dirty Bird." I had to reach into DB's cage with a broom handle to extract it for flying exercise.

In despair, I offered Dirty Bird, cage and all, to Faith if she would just take the monster off my bloodied hands. I fully outlined that DB was a filthy, unpleasant nuisance. One week later, when I arrived for my lesson, Dirty Bird was riding on Faith's shoulder, tenderly nibbling her ear, and chattering lovingly. Later Faith bought a mate for Dirty, which she named "Down."

I had no ambitions to become a professional singer. I sang with my father, who had a wonderful voice and had sung on the radio back in the days when local talent was featured. Faith had many students like me, who just wanted to learn how to enjoy singing. And, she treated us dilettantes with the same attention and respect as the notable performers, who sought her vocal coaching.

Faith may have thought I had a spark of talent that could be developed. She encouraged me to take classes at the Jean Shelton School of Acting, which was then in Berkeley, to learn better diction, emotional projection, and to build confidence. She chose a song from the 1973 musical, *Seesaw,* that was to be my signature tune, and that summed me up pretty well, "Nobody Does It Like Me."

I've got a big loud mouth,
I'm always talking much too free
If you go for tact and manners
Better stay away from me…

Paralyzing stage fright decided the matter. I could relax and enjoy myself in the serenity of Faith's music room, but the presence of a microphone, a few audience members at an open mic night, and the terror of hitting high notes, turned me to stone. Another Not Enough.

7

From Wry Irish Charmers to Pastrami on Rye

To be an Irish-born bartender in San Francisco was to be something of a king. Of course, the gift of gab, storytelling, and puckish people skills, seem born into them. The Irish I met on the trip to the old sod in the Seventies were magical people. Even farmers and working-class folks appeared connected to their history and great literary traditions in a way the American proletariat is not.

The tiny island has made outsized contributions to Western Civilization, particularly in the export, through hardships on the home ground, of its talented citizens. Because of their forlorn history, the Irish developed a remarkable, often self-deprecating, sense of humor. The playwright, Brendan Behan, said "Lord help the Irish. If it was raining soup, they'd be out with forks."

While the greeting for immigrants was harsh—No Irish Need Apply—in three cities where I've lived, New York, Boston, and San

Francisco, the Irish have been embraced and loved. On St. Patrick's Day, the saying goes, everyone is Irish. On all other days, they are great company.

In San Francisco in the 1980s, the reigning king of the City's Irish bartenders was Michael McCourt from Limerick, whose realm was primarily Perry's on Union Street. His impoverished Irish family produced a bevy of talented siblings including the Pulitzer Prize-winning author, Frank McCourt, and actor, poet, and celebrity bar owner, Malachy.

Prior to emigrating to America, Michael McCourt apprenticed as a chef at a fancy restaurant in Ireland. He recalled the experience this way "You were just nothing but a slave, a pot-washing slave. I was up to my ass in grease. I never got to cook so much as an egg."

His adventures in the USA sound like an American Dream story flavored with the Irish brand of humor. Service in the Air Force in Biloxi, Mississippi, gave him citizenship and a starting point. With the exception of a stint in Mexico with a couple buddies where the madcap plan was to start a sheep ranch, McCourt starred in bartending gigs around the country where he met and amused many celebrities.

When he was bartending in Santa Monica, he was sought out and recruited by Perry Butler who was opening a new place in San Francisco and needed a personality to anchor his bar. McCourt's wit, one-liners, and comical stories, made him a customer favorite and provided reliable quotes for Herb Caen.

Behind McCourt, in close second and third place as celebrated Irish bar men, were Seamus Coyle and Cyril Boyce, Dubliners, who both worked at WSB&G. Seamus was big in every aspect—size, personality, and wit. So big that nothing could contain him for long. He started several bars of his own, attracted followers, then unaccountably would decamp and move on. He originated the Abbey Tavern, sold it, went to work building the clientele at Perry's, started his own place, Coyles, and walked away.

Seamus could always find a bartending job. His peripatetic path took him through a couple North Beach dive bars, to the rarified atmosphere of Stars, an enterprise of celebrity chef Jeremiah Tower, and several passes through WSB&G. Irreverent to the core, Seamus taught me to genuflect the Dublin way. Piously crossing himself, touching first the forehead, then the waist, left side of the chest, then the right, he would intone "Spectacles, testicles, wallet, and watch."

The ability of Seamus, and the other High Kings of Irish bartending, to fill an entire room with their personalities, to affect the atmosphere, to infuse cordiality, and to keep folks coming back for more, was astonishing to witness. Instead of being competitive, they were a fraternity spread across the City. One year, a publication voted Seamus the Number One bartender in San Francisco. The following year, Cyril was given the same award. Acknowledging the idiocy, the friends called each other "The Two Number Ones."

Creating Best of Lists is a mainstay of city publications and often miss the real besties. Did any magazine ever note Steve Grealish of Shanghai Kelly's and other bars, as one of the All Time Best bartenders and entertainers?

Cyril was far more regular in his vocational attendance than Seamus, serving for years as the main daytime bartender and bar manager at WSB&G. Cyril's face had been assembled from props in a costume shop. An unruly mustache surmounted a snaggle-toothed grin and exuberant eyebrows tried to escape over his glasses. His brisk efficiency derived from a quarter century working for Pacific

Orient Lines. Outside of work, he shared a love for antiques with his beautiful wife, May.

One of his favorite anecdotes was about the famous actor, Micheal MacLiammoir, who was openly homosexual and scandalized Catholic Dublin by going about in full makeup and outrageous attire with his life partner, Hilton Edwards, who he met in the late 1920s. The pair, said Cyril, were known as Sodom and Begorrah.

MacLiammoir was a Brit with no Irish connections, but he moved to Ireland, learned Gaelic, and immersed himself in the culture. His contributions to Irish theater and arts were so great, he became a revered figure. I could understand his attraction to all things Irish.

Following my Irish trip, I read plays by Brendan Behan, J.M. Synge, and Sean O'Casey, the poetry of W. B. Yeats, the paintings of his brother, Jack B. Yeats, Irish history, and the music of the Chieftains, Tommy Makem, and the Clancy Brothers.

One of Cyril's story revealed his own shortcoming—handling stress with a few drinks. When May Boyce entered the hospital with labor pains, Cyril chose to handle his jitters by adjourning to a nearby bar. That ran overly long—by a couple days. He missed the birth of his son, Stephen. Seeking to make amends, he bought May a gift she'd been wanting, an electric carving knife. May thought it was a bad joke. Only then did Cyril learn Stephen had arrived via C-section.

Cyril gained another fan when Marcy Campagne was hired. She was a St Louis transplant with a shrieky, high-volume laugh, boundless exuberance, and a conversational tic of saying "I'm sorry" over inconsequential gaffes. We broke her habit by charging her a quarter every she said the word *sorry*. Then, we included her in activities we all should have apologized for.

One day, Cyril, Marcy, Arlene, and I went on a dive bar crawl in the Mission, purportedly for the historic value of the old joints. Drinks in dirty glasses were only 95 cents and we were plastered in no time. We walked into one dreary place where two or three old drunks were seated at the bar. Marcy yelled out "Drinks are on me, barkeep!"

In the time it took her to say to us "I've always wanted to do that" a hoard of old drunks emerged from the woodwork. Marcy's bar tab was under 20 dollars, but we marveled at the out-of-thin-air appearance of the boozy old dudes.

I could attest to G.K. Chesterton's observation about Irish songs:

> *The Gaels of Ireland are the men that God made mad,*
> *For all their wars are happy and all their songs are sad.*

Seamus, Cyril, and I went to pubs like Pat O'Shea's where traditional Irish music was presented and during the interludes, the audience sang popular Irish tunes. To this day, the most beautiful male voice I've heard was a working guy at The Plough and Stars on Clement, who sang a very sad, love-and-war-tinged tune "The Wind That Shakes the Barley."

> *I sat within the valley green*
> *I sat me with my true love.*
> *My sad heart strove the two between*
> *The old love and the new.*
> *The old for her, the new*
> *That made me think on Ireland dearly.*
> *While soft the wind blew down the glen*
> *And shook the golden barley.*

Seamus and Cyril both had good voices. Applied to the Irish, that may be redundant. They all seem to sing well. However, Seamus' favorite tune was not Irish, but seemed to have originated in World War II as a putdown of the Nazis. When he was sufficiently lubricated, Seamus would belt out:

Hitler had only got one ball,
Goering had one but very small.
Himmler had something similar,
But, poor old Goebbels had no balls all.

Having male friends, who were just friends, in the 1980s, was enjoyable – but tricky. The decade was a disorderly convergence of sexual mores. The Sixties' anthem "Sex, Drugs, and Rock and Roll" was still in effect. First wave Feminism rejected the need for men, fish on bicycles, and underwire bras. Second and third wave Feminism heaped on expert relationship advice that eventually created hostility between men and women that currently doesn't say "Resounding success."

Erica Jong's 1973 novel, *Fear of Flying,* introduced the concept of the "zipless fuck," which urged women to have sexual encounters with strangers without commitment or emotional attachment. Just how pointless promiscuity would advance female-friendly public policies still isn't clear. But, the concept flourished in the 1980s and supposedly empowered women, even as it ran counter to centuries of sexual norms.

In the Aristophanes' play *Lysistrata,* the women of Athens withheld sex from their men folks to make them stop warring with Sparta. There was even an axiom making the rounds in the 1980s that reflected the age-old deal between men and women: Men give love for sex. Women give sex for love. The unintended consequence of radical notions about free love and zipless fucks, was to put men in the sexual catbird seat. That's who got empowered—men—and made the 1980s their Golden Age of Getting Laid.

Adding to the confusion for women seeking relationships in San Francisco was the widely accepted belief that "all the men were gay." Supposedly, the price of living in the City was to be without a mate. I've learned to become skeptical of conventional wisdom and I questioned that defeatist attitude. I saw unattached, straight men all the time. Of course, I was working in a place that attracted men with a cornucopia of Guy Stuff—sports, good food, stiff drinks, back slapping, cleaned-up locker room joshing, and male bonding. Naturally, women followed.

From the muddle of male-female relationships in the 1980s came the idea for my first book, *Singlefile,* a guide book for women to find straight men in San Francisco. Men weren't looking for women at nail salons, flower shows, or fitness studios featuring Jane Fonda Workout videos. That's just not what they do. Women would have to seek them out. *Singlefile* would show them where to look.

In the early stages, I enlisted Sofi Kurtz to conduct interviews, which I imagined would be sprinkled through mini essays about places where men congregate. Any book (or documentary film) that is dependent on intelligent input from interviewees, is an iffy under-taking. When one woman told Sofi that she went to gay bath houses to meet men, I had to reevaluate the format. I paid Sofi for time served and concentrated on searching the city for male-centric hideouts.

My research took me to parts of the City I wouldn't have visited were I not on a mission. My appreciation of hidden treasures and resources and the people I met, increased my love for San Francisco. I thought the City looked like a beautiful cake, with swirls of frosting, resplendent on a crystal cake stand. But, when the first slice is cut and removed, there were not two layers but seven. In other words, endless delicious possibilities.

The City offered every kind of male participation sport—hang gliding, scuba diving, rugby, squash, fencing, judo, karate, darts, boxing, tennis, bowling, charter boat fishing, ice hockey, fly fishing.

Geographically, San Francisco is small. (It ain't Houston!) but, within its petite perimeters, there seemed to be everything one could want or imagine. Myriad activities, festivals, clubs, wine tasting and cooking classes, neighborhood groups, comedy clubs, museums, special events, conventions, bookstores, coffee shops, favorite male lunch spots, ballroom dancing, and more, were all awaiting women willing to try something new to find men. All the entries were introduced with commentary. Addresses, phone numbers, and contacts were provided.

When I had done enough legwork and research to nail down the basic format, I wrote a prospectus to shop *Singlefile* around to local publishers. My friend, Brian St. Pierre, who had published several books with *Chronicle Books*, thought enough of the idea to run it past them. Reportedly, the editors liked the concept, but weren't willing to take a chance on it.

Undaunted by common sense, and without a plan for marketing and distribution, I decided to self-publish *Singlefile*. Writing and publication have changed beyond recognition since the 1980s. In those days, a book was typeset and laid out for lithographic printing. Long columns of text, called *galleys,* were printed, then cut and pasted to create pages. My apartment was festooned with galleys and my art drawing table was converted to assemble pages with an Xacto knife and T-square.

With the advent of digital printing and *print on demand,* single copies of a book can be ordered, but in the 1980s, multiple copies had to be ordered based on expectation of sales. I forget how many copies I ordered. But, that number looked quite different when cardboard boxes full of freshly printed books took up every spare corner of a one-bedroom, rent-controlled apartment.

Then, there was the matter of advertising. With no internet or Amazon, book sales were dependent on print advertising, which was costly, on creating a buzz, and on persuading bookstores to give it shelf space. I persuaded two bookstores to carry *Singlefile*. I contacted the numerous singles' groups around the Bay Area offering special deals. However, I wasn't sufficiently prepared for distribution when the golden ticket came, a favorable mention from Herb Caen, via Donna Ewald.

At that time, Herb, who appreciated beautiful women, was seen around town with Donna, who was a publicist and a remarkably beautiful woman. She had a mass of dark, gold-streaked hair, Nefertiti eyes, and a fabulous wardrobe wrapped around a voluptuous figure. To make matters worse, she was a generous and likeable person. One evening, while I was waiting on Herb and Donna, she mentioned to him that I'd written a book. Shortly thereafter, Herb's column noted my book "…[A] breezy good read."

That prompted Ed to say "Well, I guess we'd better have it here." Self-promotion made me squirmy and was on my Not Enough list. So, it was oddly unsettling to see bar patrons leafing through my book, as it was being relentlessly flogged by bartender, Neil Riofski. That noble-hearted soul celebrated every small step I took towards becoming a writer. Several times, I begged Neil to write, too. "I'm a lightweight, Neil. I know you can do this." He always agreed to try.

I may have recouped the cost of the book's production. In other words, no profit. But, publishing *Singlefile* paid dividends in other ways. It brought my writing to the attention of local editors and I made several TV appearances. One was to be a location shot presented by local TV reporter, Jill Rappaport, which would feature a place to find single men.

I chose the legendary Financial District water hole, Templebar, secured permission to film, and (because I'd been paying attention to Ed Moose) I rounded up 6-8 highly desirable and well-spoken men to ensure a good selection.

When Jill, who was single, entered the bar, her eyes lit up at Dude Bonanza. Rather than approach any of my well-prepped guys, she put the microphone in front of a dreary Financial District dullard with his nose in a glass of bourbon. Brightly, she asked "Is this a good place for women to meet men?"

His surly response "Nope." ...Ah, the best laid plans.

A guy, who ran a singles' club in the Bay Area, which was widely advertised in the *Bay Guardian* and elsewhere, blew me off when I tried to interest him in *Singlefile*. A year later, he contacted me and wanted to enter a partnership to "franchise" my concept in cities all over the country. (*Singlefile Knoxville?*) Doing the same thing over and over had no appeal. Nor did being professionally single. I told him the concept was his for the taking.

Singlefile lead to a gig with *San Francisco Magazine* via a friend of Sofi's named Martha Jo Policastro, who was seeking a writing partner for food-related articles. Jo had been an airline stewardess in the days when her stunning good looks and high-wattage smile were job requirements. She had traveled the world with the airlines and spent several years learning the culinary arts at a school in Paris.

By the 1980s, she was determined to Be Somebody in the San Francisco restaurant scene, which she accomplished a number of times. During our collaboration, she was the manager or working partner of Bentley's, a seafood restaurant, that featured an extravagant, rowboat-sized display of shrimp, crab, raw oysters and other brine-y exotica snugged into mounds of gleaming ice.

Her energy and ambition were non-stop. She had an impressive network of resources and contacts, including someone at *San Francisco Magazine,* so we were able to get started quickly. We did about six articles together and my wacky turn-of-mind soon led me to humorous takes on the mania of California cuisine at the time.

It was after all, the advent of *garlic encrusted duck livers en Croute in a reduction of beaks and feet* served on a vast plate garnished with baby nasturtiums.

I doubt Jo appreciated my impertinence, but we managed to pull off a memorable event, the Great Cross-Country Deli Derby. As everyone knows, who has been around ex-pat New Yorkers, they always bemoan the absence of great delicatessens and the corned beef, pastrami, and rye breads they claim only the Big Apple can produce. We decided to test the theory with a blind tasting between New York and San Francisco delicatessens.

The crazy scheme was that Jo and I would fly to New York for a weekend, gather products from three delis, fly back to San Francisco where products from three local delis would await, and a mixed panel of East and West Coast experts would judge the entries. We figured Max's Opera Café on Van Ness was our City's best candidate, but we weren't even sure if New York's premiere delis, Stage and Carnegie, would be on board with the contest.

To facilitate our whirlwind junket, Jo, who was familiar with New York, and, of course, had contacts, hired a car and driver. That's a grand way of describing a young Middle Eastern man with an older Pontiac, but the guy knew his city well and could deliver and retrieve us, curb side, at the places we needed to be. Jo wanted to check out the latest food trends, hot restaurants de jour, and a few classics.

We hit Petrossian's for champagne and caviar, a tapas bar where we ate baby eels, the Russian Tea Room for the glitzy décor, and drinks at a nightclub called Chinoise, where we saw Geraldo Rivera. (In any decade, it may have been impossible to visit NYC without seeing Geraldo.) I managed a side trip to the Metropolitan Museum of Art and the Guggenheim while Jo did more tasty research.

Our products had been ordered and purchased, then we hit a snag. Leo Steiner, the hands-on owner of Carnegie Deli was in-it-to-win-it. Rather than letting us collect his items ahead of time, Leo insisted on delivering his products to our hotel the day of our departure, which was a 7 a.m. flight. We had a sleepless night stressing about all the details that had to come together and the huge glitch if Carnegie Deli missed the mark.

At 6 a.m., there was a knock on our hotel door, a voice called out "Carnegie Deli," and Leo himself handed us several shopping bags emitting the aroma of freshly baked light and dark rye breads, and the scent of warm corned beef and pastrami. We checked our luggage through, but carried our precious cargo aboard and stowed the bags in the overhead compartments—where the tantalizing fragrances filled the cabin and tormented our hungry fellow travelers, who looked at us reproachfully as they opened tiny bags of peanuts.

Amazingly, the mad scheme came together on both ends of the country. We notified Leo Steiner (and one other person) that Carnegie Deli had won by a mile and New York's reputation for deli supremacy was justified. A week or so later, we received a cheerful note from the other person, Mayor Ed Koch.

8

Tyrants, Hoodlums, & Kitchen Saints

Everyone was fascinated with WSB&G and an article about the famous waterhole was sure to find a publisher. Thus, I sold a piece to San Francisco Magazine which explored the notion that WSB&G was a "family." Of the sort, I joked, that would arise from marriages between the Marx Brothers and the Borgias. Ed Moose, who rarely spoke to me directly, approached me to say, with a furrowed brow, that Clay Felker had read and praised the piece.

I was so taken aback at a show of tepid interest from Ed, that I could only squeak out "Oh, good." I wisely refrained from asking "Who is Clay Felker?" Not recognizing the name of the legendary editor, who originated the modern city magazine format, would have destroyed any brief credibility I earned with Ed.

Another person, who sought to write about WSB&G, was introduced to the staff as Myra. Our assistance in providing insight and anecdotes to her was requested. The first commandment of writing is "Write what you know," which can happen in two ways: research the hell out of the subject—or live it. Myra was attempting the first method, but the weird and complicated world of restaurants and staff, the sights, the smells, the interaction of workers in the kitchen, the front of the house, and dealing with the public, can only be lived.

Offering assistance to Myra, I felt, was supposed to be my job since I was exhibiting faint signs of becoming a writer. My files consisted of notes on cocktail napkins that were tossed in a shoebox. Although I didn't foresee any actual use for the notes, I was covetous of my experiences and didn't share with Myra.

What I couldn't possibly impart to Myra was the path through kitchens and dining rooms all over the country that had preceded my arrival at WSB&G. My first job was at Litchfield Farmhouse in my Florida hometown, a restaurant with long, waist-high freezer cabinets with multiple doors for five-gallon containers of ice cream. Hand-dipped cones and sundaes were the most popular items, but orders for hand-packed pints or quarts would require a freezer-burn dive into the cabinets. And, the busier I was with other orders, the more likely the request would be for a pint of Pistachio, the hardest substance in the world.

I'm indebted to the manager of Litchfield Farmhouse, a tall handsome graduate student, for teaching me an exotic swear word that became my favorite, and which came in handy when hacking frozen pistachio—and ever after.

Most food servers, or waitresses and waiters as we known in less gender-conscious days, probably started in a place like Litchfield's where the smell of the grill permeated the air, a mixed aroma of sizzling hamburger patties, grilled cheese, and French fries roiling in the fryer basket. Occasionally, we'd be asked to step in for the grill cook and wield the long, hamburger flipper spatula and scrape the golden, meat-flecked grease into the mysterious opening in the grill's surface. How could that be conveyed to Myra?

In those days, long before California cuisine produced celebrity chefs, anyone who cooked, whether a short-order cook in a greasy apron and a paper hat or a classically trained chef in a tall white toque, was likely to be a tyrant. Such was the case with Chef John, who commanded one of the largest kitchens I've ever seen, at a country club in Salem, Massachusetts, where my college roomie and I worked one summer.

Chef John's realm consisted of a fully-equipped bakery, another area for *garde manger* (the cold items, salads, fancy appetizers, and decorative flourishes) then, a galley for the line cooks and the *sous chef*, and, finally grand central where Chef John expedited the orders and inspected every plate. All those areas were connected with stainless steel tracks upon which the food servers slid large trays that would be loaded with plates, covered with stainless steam covers, and carried shoulder-high to the dining room.

Chef John was ferocious and utterly intolerant of even the slightest glitch in procedure. As most of us were college students learning the trade, glitches were not uncommon. Once, he became so enraged about a small error, he rushed to the line of servers, brandishing a French carving knife, and with a flick of the blade, slit the buttons off the offending waiter's jacket. The rest of us were stricken with terror as the buttons bounced on the floor.

Our respite from Chef John's tyranny came after lunch was served, and we had a break before dinner preparations began. We would congregate in the employee's parking to chat or to listen to music on car radios, which eventually led to dance lessons. Mark was a tall, slim, young black man, who was attending Dartmouth on a scholarship, "Academic, not basketball" as he would point out. Mark was appalled at the state of dance moves among the white staffers.

He introduced us to the music of Wilson Pickett, Sam and Dave, Isley Brothers, Temptations, and other Sixties' artists. At the end of the summer, as we were all about to disperse for home, Mark organized a dance party at a black nightclub in Roxbury and pronounced our moves sufficiently acceptable to be exported to our respective colleges.

Another college job was at Patricia Murphy's Candlelight Restaurant in Deerfield Beach, Florida, which sought to deliver gourmet food on a mass scale in a remarkable setting. It was lodged in a huge building with a towering, vaulted roof that was fitted with translucent panels. The interior had elevated walkways over splashing waterways that led to cozy dining areas surrounded by living trees and tropical shrubs. The tables, covered with starched linen and napkins, silver and glassware gleaming with candle glow, made for an impressive atmosphere—that was also alive.

As I placed a cup of vichyssoise in front of a patron, I saw a little green tree frog launch itself from a palm tree and land in the cup. His yellow eyes peered up from the thick white soup. Thankfully, it wasn't hot soup, which gave me time to say I'd brought the wrong item, whisk away the little guy, and release it downstream and out of sight.

The breakfast cook at Aspen Meadows Resort was another tyrant. The resort hosts gatherings of the Aspen Institute, which has become the Davos of the Rockies, but always attracted celebrity visitors to Aspen, Colorado. The breakfast kitchen and cozy dining area were separate from the main kitchen and formal dining room, and was operated by an attractive young woman whose autocratic manner suggested that making pancakes was on par with brain surgery.

One morning, Eric Sevareid, the esteemed newsman, appeared at the breakfast kitchen with a fish. He had gotten up early, visited a nearby stream with his fly rod, and hooked a nice rainbow trout.

He asked politely if he might have it cooked for his breakfast. I relayed the query to the cook, who flatly refused, saying the trout would foul her grill.

We weren't busy, the trout could be pan fried, and she was just being a jerk, wielding her little power to the detriment of hospitality. I took the fish to the main kitchen, gutted, and cooked it. I still remember how pleased Mr. Sevareid was. Always respect the man/fish bond.

Job opportunities in Aspen were scarce. Housing was hen's teeth. Scarcity made for landlords and employers, who were tyrants. Hubert Earhardt was rumored to fall in the tyrant category. An Austrian-born immigrant, he was chef/owner of The Golden Horn restaurant where he served up classic French and traditional Austrian cuisine. He had an opening for a pantry chef whose *garde manger* duties included fancy appetizers and desserts, salad dressings that were made from scratch, and plate decorations like radish roses, carrot curls, and tomato roses.

I had zero experience with garde manger, which I admitted to him, also that I badly needed a job. I told Hubert that my German grandfather had been a chef and I was willing to learn. The notion that food preparation was in my DNA was less persuasive than the still vacant position and the rapidly approaching winter season. Hubert was willing to teach me as long as I caught on the first time.

The most obnoxious task of my life was preparing escargot. The snails came in, what we called a #10 can, packed in a vile smelling liquid that could only be removed from my hands by vigorous scrubbing with lemon wedges. (Even so, stray cats seemed drawn to me.) After rinsing the snails, I had to stuff them into reuseable shells, leaving room for a generous scoop of garlic butter, which I mixed from Hubert's recipe.

When an order came in, I'd place six of the refrigerated escargots on a small round metal tray with indentations and hand them off to Hubert, who put the dish under the broiler. While there are other escargot preparations, eating them from their shells is a ritual-laden custom with traditional tongs for holding the shells and curved two-tine forks for extracting the snail, and with extra French bread for mopping up the delicious garlic butter.

My attempts at Baked Alaska taxed Hubert's one-lesson rule. The dessert begins with a layer of sponge or pound cake topped with a couple scoops of ice cream and piped with meringue from a pastry bag. The meringue must completely seal the contents or the ice cream will melt when dessert is popped in the oven to quickly brown the meringue.

Anthony was Hubert's maître d'. He was a handsome, snooty Brit, who wore a tuxedo with Cary Grant elegance. Anthony would flambe the Baked Alaska with brandy at tableside. Thus, three of us had to coordinate, usually at the busiest time, and the showy presentation would set off a flurry of orders, something we all dreaded.

My early Baked Alaskas were unsatisfactory. I didn't know how to use the pastry bag to good effect. Hubert was annoyed and said "Here at Golden Horn, Baked Alaska is supposed to look like a tall, elegant, sailing ship. Yours look like a barge!"

Eventually, I got the knack and learned to perform the many duties of the pantry so efficiently that Hubert allowed me to set my own hours. Ski as long as you want, he said, just get your work done. Being prepared, with ample quantities of all ingredients and sauces, is essential in busy restaurants. When the doors open, it's off to the races, with no time to backfill an omission.

Experienced chefs like Hubert could quickly detect a problem. I was fond of my Austrian tyrant and wouldn't disabuse his trust with shoddy work. We worked together in companionable silence most of the time. Hubert was married to a beautiful, younger, woman, who had been an Austrian ski champion, and spent all day on the mountain. His part of our companionable silence was worrying about who Trudi was with out on the black diamond trails. Mine was trying to focus on a job I quite enjoyed.

Frequently, bartenders are tyrants. In restaurant hierarchy, bartenders rank well below chefs, but way ahead of wait staff. They can ignore harried servers at the service bar anxious for cocktail orders to be filled while they are chatting up women at the bar they hope to take to bed. Sexual activity is a constant in a business where food arouses pleasure centers and alcohol reduces inhibitions. Co-workers, who confront tyrant bartenders that are on the prowl, can just make matters worse for themselves. But, sometimes a propitious moment comes…

In the 1970s, I was working at Ken's Pub in Boston. The head bartender was a graceless clod, whose only qualification for the job seemed to be friendship with the owner, also a graceless clod. The likelihood of the Mr. Bigshot Bartender going home with any of the hotties he wooed across the plank was next to zero. Yet, he refused to treat cocktail orders from waitresses queued at the service bar with any urgency.

It was customary for food servers to cash in their tips, coins and small bills, at the end of the evening. Mr. Big Shot wouldn't do it, as that would mean more work for him, counting the change and reconciling his cash drawer with sales. I organized a plan with the other women. We held back our change until the day came that Mr. Big Shot desperately needed change to keep the bar running. Then, a deal for better treatment was struck.

Mr. Big Shot fancied himself a high flyer, which is common in a profession where one may leave work with hundreds of dollars in their pocket. When I announced I was taking a second job to earn money for a trip to Europe, he asked me how much I planned to save. I said two thousand dollars. He replied "How long are you going to stay—15 minutes?"

One of the waitresses at Ken's Pub jumped right into the sexual possibilities when Wilt Chamberlain came into the restaurant. She made a beeline for the notoriously promiscuous NBA star and took him home. We were all surprised by that as she seemed rather prim and proper. The next day, propriety had reasserted itself and the only reply she made to our inquiring looks was to say "In proportion."

The second job, which commenced after my night shift at Ken's Pub, was at a coffee shop in a motel on Beacon Street. Surprisingly, it was the only place still open after the bars closed and was popular with bar and restaurant workers, who like to unwind with a bite to eat before heading home. Among the late-nighters, was Rudy Guarino, the owner of the famous Sugar Shack night club on Boylston Street, always with an entourage. They were rumored to be the Boston Mafia, which supplemented income from the night club side and concerts at Sugar Shack with stolen goods that went out the back door. Rudy and crew were always served by Kate Sullivan, a charming Irish immigrant, who deftly accommodated their requests.

Nevertheless, I came to the attention of two of Rudy's crew. One was a young hoodlum, who flirted by urging me to shop at the Sugar Shack where he said wonderful things were available at a third the usual price. Or, as he said "A toid."

Kate advised me that I would be safe from mafia entanglements, as long as I didn't owe anyone a favor. So, I always declined the shopping invitation, which was so perplexing to the hoodlum, he would look at me, shrug his shoulders, and say "A toid."

My other admirer was a shambling, older fellow named Gigilo (pronounced jee-jello) whose exact function in the Mob I didn't want to know. He once brought his wife along to meet me and the two of them reminisced happily about climbing down the fire escape on their building when the police were beating on their door.

Gigilo had an inquiring but disconnected mind. I wondered what he might have become had he not been born into a certain kind of life. He informed me that the White Cliffs of Dover were supposedly comprised of tiny marine animals. Did I think that was possible?

Those kinds of questions came up on a coin-operated quiz machine in the lobby of the coffee shop. Each player would insert a quarter, then a question would pop up, and the first person to hit a button with the correct answer won that round. Gigilo won all the sports' questions. I won all the literature questions.

It was such a regular feature for us that Gigilo brought a pocket full of slugs for the quiz machine, so I could save my quarters for the trip fund. When it was time to leave on my European adventure, Gigilo pressed a hundred-dollar bill into my hand and said "When you get to dem White Cliffs of Dover, you find out about dem little marine animals and send old Gigilo a postcard."

My first job in Boston was a camera equipment store that had a photo processing lab. Tony Conigliaro appeared one day with an unusual request. The beloved, but ill-fated Red Sox player had taken a picture of the moon with his 35 mm camera. He asked if the photo could be enlarged to show what was on the surface of the moon. Tony C didn't get to the major leagues by studying astronomy.

Another unforgettable customer was an older, wealthy, Jewish lady, always richly dressed, whose hair was professionally sculpted into a glistening, tangerine-colored beehive. She was pleasant, and I vaguely considered that her whole life must have been one of comfort and privilege—until the day she reached for the packet containing her photos. The sleeve of her mink coat slid aside revealing a number tattooed on her forearm.

Loops get closed…In the early 1990s, when I was a columnist at The Oakland Tribune, I met Bob Cochnar, the husband of Myra, the would-be WSB&G writer. Cochnar was a lifelong newsman, with postings all around the country, who was part of management at the Trib. As such, I didn't have much contact with him. But, when he temporarily served as Editor, we discovered we were both Trivia, Jeopardy, useless information accumulators. An email competition with the waggish newsman ensued.

Cochnar once mentioned Humpty Dumpty in connection with *Alice in Wonderland.* I bet him $50 that Humpty wasn't in Alice. I completely forgot that Humpty Dumpty is a character in *Through the Looking Glass.* Technically, I was right, but I paid up anyway for a valuable lesson about being so focused on one answer that I missed other possibilities.

I had more than met my match, rarely won a contest with Bob, and jokingly asked him "Is there anything you don't know?"

Cochnar replied "It's possible I may have forgotten the ingredients in a Sidecar."

Kitchen tyrants were virtually absent from WSB&G, in large part because the bulwarks of food preparation were two saints. Manuel Sauceda and Edgar Rojas were Mexican immigrants. They had started as dishwashers at Pistola's, then understudied as youngsters with Pistola's chef Aldo Persich, who was impressed with their work ethic. When Sam and Ed bought the place, the two hard working cooks joined the new venture.

Manuel's battered face reflected the boxer he once was. His rough exterior was wrapped around a generous, patient soul. His ability to remain cool and unflustered in the midst of chaos made him the anchor of the kitchen.

Edgar Rojas, who was younger than Manuel, had a beautiful golden face like a Toltec mask. He, too, was steady under fire. Together, the two of them turned out massive amounts of food, wielding countless sauté pans over the leaping blue flames of the range top. Every night, a rhythm was set as orders came in, were prepared, and sent out. We all dreaded the inevitable glitches or mistakes that interrupted the rhythm: An incorrect order. A returned item. Or a customer who wanted their pasta *al dente.*

Frequently-ordered pastas, like fettucine, spaghetti, penne, farfalle, were pre-cooked to al dente, portioned into plastic bags, then dumped into boiling water to quickly fill orders. Hand-made pastas for specials were cooked to order. But, the occasional demand for toothier al dente created an extra step that took one of the cooks out of the rhythm and slowed the entire process.

Thus, we food servers were dismayed when we had to ask these soldiers of sauté for a redo or special preparation. Manuel, whose English was limited to kitchen-ese, would listen patiently to my problem, as he did with everyone, then, put one of his huge boxer paws on my shoulder, and say "S'okay, Yudy."

Alan Goldman was a kitchen disrupter. He was a New York transplant, a former ad man, small in stature, large in aggression, who had a gleaming bald head and fashionable wardrobe. He carried a leather man purse with a shoulder strap, which gave the impression he kept important work close to hand. I suspected it contained a bottle of Johnny Walker Black. He was a prodigious scotch drinker, which exacerbated his foul personality. He once announced he'd given up drinking, which translated to switching from scotch to copious amounts of beer and wine.

When Goldman was well-oiled, it was time to dine. Jabbing his fore finger for emphasis, he insisted that his spaghetti must be al dente. Oblivious to the slowdowns he created in the kitchen, Goldman was known to send back his al dente order if it wasn't al dente enough and demand a redo. The staff considered dumping a package of dry, store-bought spaghetti, covered with Marinara sauce, on a plate and serving it to him.

Eventually, Goldman wrangled his way into a food critics' job. That was one of the most coveted of the scarce writing jobs in the City and probably set off a firestorm of envy among freelance food writers. But, in contrast to his abrasive persona, Goldman's food writing was sensitive, engaging, and suggested he was a charming dinner companion. The package and the contents don't always match.

Occasionally, Mary Etta felt the need to hire a name chef or an up-and-comer to revamp the menu or to add some California cuisine cache to the WSB&G kitchen. Manuel and Edgar would dutifully learn the *arriviste's* recipes, fold those methods into their existing skills, and carry on holding together the whole kitchen side of the operation.

Did they know how much we loved them? They didn't drink or dawdle after work to chat, so the conventional ways of showing appreciation in bar settings weren't available. Personal tributes like gifts or money weren't appropriate. So, there's a grey area of Not Enough among co-workers when some parties contribute so much to the overall effort—and gratitude can't find the right expression.

9

Writers & Writer-ing

Writers were particularly esteemed at Washington Square Bar & Grill. In part, the newspaper writing Ed Moose had done in his younger days, and his natural facility for language, fed his appreciation of writers. An educated and well-read staff was particularly accommodating to word wranglers. Moreover, San Francisco itself seemed especially enthusiastic about the craft, which often drew upon the City's unique character and geography for material, even claiming writers like Daishell Hammett, Jack Keroac, and Mark Twain, whose connections were tenuous or transient.

Mark Twain's observation "The coldest winter I ever spent was a summer in San Francisco" was invoked constantly, along with endless replays of Tony Bennett's song "I Left My Heart in San Francisco." The only way to stay sane amid the constant repetition was to put those in the same category as grandparent stories told at Thanksgiving. A degree of tolerance meant you were part of the family.

Given the high regard for writers, there were relatively few places to be published. *San Francisco Magazine* was the kind of eponymous publication all cities and regions feel obliged to produce. However, the city magazine got serious competition from *San Francisco In Focus,* which was the monthly membership publication of KQED, the local station for the Public Broadcasting Service. *In Focus* had grown from a television guide into a regular magazine competing for the same readership as *San Francisco Magazine* but with the advantage of revenue from PBS supporters.

Other options were *California Living,* a newsprint magazine insert in the combined Sunday edition of the *Chronicle* and *Examiner.* Subsequently, *California Living* was replaced by the glossy *Image Magazine.* And, there was the *Bay Guardian,* the so called "alternative press," which is a feature of most metro areas that combines progressive politics, muckraking, and coverage of music and entertainment. I called it Leftist politics and Righteous entertainment.

The limited places to be published in San Francisco were defended by editors, who had stables of dependable writers and little time to read queries from wannabes. The situation was very frustrating for an aspiring writer, but in retrospect, it was commendable in some ways, primarily because the quality of writing was assured. Nowadays, social media, blogs, and online publications, provide unlimited choices for readers and the writing quality may be appallingly bad. So bad as to recall a famous putdown by Truman Capote. Asked what he thought of the writing of popular poet Rod McKuen, Capote tartly replied "That's not writing, that's typing."

Hal Silverman was the editor of *California Living.* As such, he was a powerful figure in the City's publishing scene. His presence in a room full of writers would set off a scramble to touch the hem of his garment. Considering Silverman's exalted position, it's amazing that my first-ever article appeared in *California Living*—even with a boost from influential friends. It was a profile of Jeanie Kortum's adventures in Greenland with Inuit people and her resultant novel, *Ghost Vision.*

Jeanie L. Kortum was the daughter of Karl Kortum, a much-esteemed figure, who founded the National Maritime Historical Park at Aquatic Park. Its collection of historic vessels included her namesake, a clipper ship named the *Jeanie Landles.* She was a quirky person, who traveled to remote locations to learn and write about isolated people and their tribal practices. The discipline needed to do that seemed at odds with Jeanie's disorganized, goofball handling of her daily affairs.

To interview Jeanie about her polar adventure, I met with her at the Kortum family farm in Petaluma. Upon arrival, she opened an oversized purse, withdrew a white rabbit, attached a leash to its harness, and staked it out in the yard. From a window, I watched nervously as the rabbit nibbled grass and hawks circled in the blue sky above.

In later years, Jeanie's novel *Stones* documented life with hunter-gatherers in Kenya. But, her greatest achievement may have been her humanitarian work on behalf of homeless youth in San Francisco. She pulled together community resources to create a program called A Home Away from Homelessness.

Dugald Stermer, did the *Ghost Vision* illustration for the novel and the cover of *California Living.* And, I believe, a good word from Brian St. Pierre to Silverman was helpful in getting me the gig. In other words, I had an incredibly lucky launch.

Silverman told me about a cocktail party of local literati that I should attend to get acquainted. At the party, I secured a glass of white wine, assumed the classic wallflower position, and wondered how getting acquainted was supposed to happen. I noticed a beard-and-glasses, professorial type, making his way from female to female in the gathering and he eventually fetched up in front of me. It was well-known writer, Herb Gold. He asked me who I was and why I was there. I related I'd just been published and "hopefully" would be again. Gold sniffed dismissively, said "Hopefully is not a word," and walked away.

Changes in usage of the English language, usually decried as declining, have been a topic for a long time. (How would the modern tech world operate if we still spoke like Geoffrey Chaucer?) The rule that a sentence should not end with a preposition had been handily dealt with by Winston Churchill, who said "This is the type of errant pedantry up with which I will not put."

Apparently, Gold was still in the errant pedantry business regarding *hopefully,* which is an adverb, and, in the plummeting state of the English language, may be used to describe an action. Nevertheless, I was so stung by the shibboleth sheriff that, to this day, seeing the word *hopefully* brings on a panic attack.

In the mid-1980s, a phenomenon rattled the magazine publishing industry. That phenom' was Tina Brown. The Brit was hired to reinvent the moribund *Vanity Fair* magazine, which had sales of 200,000 when she took over and was successfully boosted to 1.2 million. Brown was described as "…[A] once in a lifetime creative force in a business that generally rewarded dull incompetence."

The revamped *Vanity Fair* was a daring mix of celebrity profiles, fashion, murders most foul, foreign and domestic reporting, amazing photography from the likes of Annie Leibovitz, and fragrant with scratch and sniff perfume ads.

Suddenly, all the San Francisco editors were saying "We want to be the next *Vanity Fair.*" What that actually meant was they wanted the advertising revenue of *Vanity Fair,* not so much that they were willing to try unconventional content. Given the chance to publish yet another article about Ed Moose, they would choose Moose over a profile of some of the City's unrecognized talent. Those were the people who interested me. Occasionally, I was able to persuade an editor to OK an offbeat piece.

One such, featured twin sisters, who operated a downtown cosmetics' store. Unlike the snooty service of cosmetic counters in department stores, the twins swarmed women, who entered their shop, with a flurry of products and colors and makeup tips. The twins were from Indianapolis and I likened the swarm to a pit crew at the Indy 500. The atmosphere combined slumber-party-shenanigans with the attentions of mad Mary Kay reps determined to win a pink Cadillac. It was great gal fun.

Another article featured Chris Pray, a multi-talented funny guy. He was a comedian and improv veteran of The Committee. But, he was also a puppeteer, who created a KRON TV program for children called *Buster and Me,* which had won five Emmy awards for children's programming. While interviewing Chris in his small North Beach apartment, I noted the gilded statuettes everywhere, including one Emmy being used as a doorstop, which I mentioned in the article.

After publication, Chris received a stern letter from the Television Academy stating they would take away his Emmys if he didn't treat them with more respect. I was mortified to have caused harm to Chris, but also exasperated at the panties-in-a-wad pomposity of an Academy, which presumes to recognize comedic talent without understanding where comedy comes from.

For Chris, humor was a release from a childhood of health problems and taunting from other kids. Without humor, what are the other options? Depression? Despair? Rage?

While some of my articles passed muster, some did not. Through my brother, Jeff Berkley, who was a globe-trotting submarine pilot and engineer, I secured an interview with Sylvia Earle, a world renown marine biologist, oceanographer, and author, who lived in the East Bay. The magazine I pitched it to, failed to bite, which must have been my fault, certainly not the subject of the profile.

Another failure-to-launch article was meant to support the return of a major equine event to Golden Gate Park, that being Grand Prix Show

Jumping, a sport the general public usually only sees on the televised Summer Olympics. One of the proponents for the event was a wealthy woman, who operated a saddlery in the City, near Golden Gate Park.

At that time, horses were still boarded in the Park and lessons could be booked, so a saddle/tack shop was not incongruous. I had taken a lesson at the Park stables from pompous riding instructor on a horse I was told was 42 years old, which I later learned should have qualified for horse-longevity in the Guinness Book of Records.

When I arrived at the saddlery for our appointment to discuss the potential horse event, the well-to-do woman was on the phone, giving off a pretentious vibe by talking to another society type about P.L.U (People Like Us). Her considerably younger husband was slouched in a chair listening to her with a look of disdain on his handsome face. I felt like I'd walked into a scene between the kind of awkward, mis-matched couples in Jane Austen novels.

I came away with contact information for a couple in Woodside, who hoped to compete their $100,000 jumper in the event. I traveled to their farm for an interview and took photos of the leaping horse. The package didn't convince editors that readers would be interested. However, the episode gave me a glimpse into a world I would later write about extensively, the horse industry, which is as quirky and character-filled as the saloon business.

Fortunately, I met a number of writers who were not cut from the spirit-crushing Herb Gold mold. One of my favorites was Michael Koepf, who usually appeared at the Washington Square Bar & Grill in the company of two other novelists, Chuck Kinder and Max Crawford. The rumpled, long haired, bearded trio looked like three grizzly bears, who got tangled in a lumberjack's clothesline, then went out for a night of hard drinking.

Mike grew up in a family of commercial fishermen, served as a Green Beret, and found his way to novel writing. He lived on a mountain in Mendocino with his then wife, Mary, in a hand-built cabin adjacent to a writing studio situated inside a gigantic wine cask. He gave fabulous parties. His first novel, *Save the Whale,* published in 1978, was a humorous take on the tree-hugging, environmentalist attitudes, and their potential for exploitation that were to overwhelm California in the years to come.

I once asked Mike about his experiences as a fisherman. He cocked his head and said "Do you mean Ernest Hemingway romance-of-the-sea fishing? Or commercial fishing? Which is hours and hours of monotony interspersed with moments of hideous terror."

Another time I asked Mike his opinion of a story idea. He listened thoughtfully and replied, "It's a good idea and here's my advice: Don't ever tell a good idea to another writer."

Joan Ryan was an *Examiner* sports' writer and already breaking barriers as one of the first female sports' columnists. She would go on to cover every major sporting event, win numerous awards, and write a hugely significant book, *Little Girls in Pretty Boxes: Making and Breaking of Elite Gymnasts and Figure Skaters.* She continues to explore new areas with her writing and to accumulate accolades.

We had both grown up in Florida in the years before the state became a concrete-covered destination for snowbirds. As such, we were familiar with Florida's pervasive critter population, including the cockroach, which was wryly referred to as Florida's state bird. That early exposure to creepie crawlies made for unflappable women.

Thus, we were having lunch at Perry's on Union Street when we saw a cockroach crawling on a wall near our table. We didn't react, but went on eating. The incongruity struck us at the same moment. We looked at each other, burst into giggles, and simultaneously said "Florida!"

As I became acquainted with more writers, it seemed there are people who choose writing and people, who are chosen by writing. The choosers often come from the academic side and the chosen from life experiences. One of my favorite college art instructors, a successful painter named Sandra Marchetti, observed a student working on a failed painting, and said "You shouldn't be in art if you don't have anything to say."

The raw material of *something to say* in writing can come from academia or from life. What's fascinating is to see how the raw material is shaped by the craft of writing. Of the writers I've met, Brian St. Pierre was the most enamored with the craft. He was born in New Bedford, Massachusetts, interned in the family restaurant business, attended Boston University, heeded the Go-West-Young-Man clarion, dabbled in acting, became a writer and wine expert, and when I met him, was public relations director of the Wine Institute, a trade organization for the California wine industry.

Brian was a tall shambling figure with a rough-hewn face, and a mop of black hair starting to silver. He was a devotee of the Washington Square Bar & Grill, but our paths seldom crossed. He and his wife, Jackie, were part of the Sunday brunch crowd, who enjoyed leisurely hours reading newspapers and chatting with others.

Breakfast and brunch, I believe, are the most difficult food services. A poached egg quickly loses credibility if it's not delivered speedily. Waiters may be responsible for toasting English muffins to coordinate with the eggs and Hollandaise from the cooks for Eggs Benedict, while hustling Bloody Marys and Mimosas. Not being a morning person, I avoided Sunday brunch duties at WSB&G.

So, I wasn't well acquainted with Brian, although he was a longtime fan of the saloon. That changed when a postcard from Brian appeared on the staff bulletin board. He was on a business trip someplace with frigid temperatures and joked about the prospect of eating the sled dogs.

I asked Sam about the postcard and Brian. "Is he funny?" I asked. Sam, whose praise of most people was faint, assured me that Brian was funny, smart, well-read, sociable, and he noted with heavy emphasis "Divorced now."

The catalogue of Brian's good qualities was even wider. He was generous, patient, and kind. He was mentor and cheerleader. He believed I had talent for writing and shared his love of the craft and contacts. More than anyone or anything, he helped to fill the empty space of Not Enough that I'd lived with most of my life.

When I was very young, 5-6 years old, I ran away from home, the way that children frustrated by small events often do. My mother followed me down the street where we lived. She could have said a number of things:

We are a family, we need you.
Whatever the problem is, we can work it out.
You are my child and I love you.

Instead, she said "It's okay for you to leave, but you must return everything I've given you." And, right there on the street, where our neighbors could see, she had me remove my little girl shoes, the little white socks with lace at the top, my shorts and shirt. When I was stripped down to cotton panties imprinted with teddy bears, I capitulated. From that moment on, eviscerated of self-hood, I was a puppet upon which she projected her unfulfilled dreams and thwarted ambitions.

As long as I was under her roof, she controlled every aspect of my life. She made my clothes, cut my hair, pushed me into activities I was shy about, and demanded complete obedience. In one instance she decided what my science fair project would be, made it herself, had me submit it, and collect an award, so I could add *fraud* to my empty resume. Often, I would lie in bed at night, seething with rage, praying for the day I would be free of her control, but fearful of the physical enforcement that would result if I rebelled too soon.

By my mid-twenties, I was emancipated—physically—but not mentally. I was attending college, financing classes by working in bars, and outwardly functioning well. But, I was drinking too much, subject to explosive episodes of anger, and engaging in behaviors my mother would have hated. That situation might have gone on with no end in sight, until I began to hallucinate.

In unexpected moments, usually in small places, I would see a marionette hanging motionless in a tangle of strings. Unseen hands were no longer operating the marionette directly, but without the empowering hands, the manikin was incapable of self-actualization. Those brief glimpses were terrifying. I became claustrophobic, but I couldn't avoid every circumstance where my inert doppelgänger might suddenly appear. The hallucinations became more frequent until I was nearly paralyzed with fear.

I found a good psychiatrist, who helped me identify the issues. After one year of weekly consults at ninety bucks a pop, the marionette was gone. Another year of analysis might have averted decades of banging around the Pinball Machine of Life still reacting to my phobia about control. Instead, I resolved I would not enter a profession or a job or living arrangement or relationship that gave others authority over me. That aversion to control, the need to protect my prerogatives at all costs, made for self-centeredness that could be cruel and unfeeling.

At dinner, I broke off an engagement with a fiancé because he suggested I shouldn't have a second dinner roll before the arrival of the entrée. I decided I'd never get engaged again. Marriage looked like a prison.

If I'd continued with therapy, the shrink might have helped me identify and resist the perennial problem areas that plagued most of my life:

You will lack self-confidence in all you do and underrate whatever success you have.

You will seek validation in sexual affairs, but strong-arm actual love.

You will not maintain your friendships because you can't imagine you have any real value to anyone.

Such was the mental patient in remission that Brian adopted. His love for writing reawakened the interest I'd abandoned so long ago and laid to rest any thought of pursuing art or singing. His compassion and support helped me envision a future that had some direction.

Most of Brian's books and articles, lively with humor and anecdotes, are devoted to wine and food. On one occasion, I sought to test his wine expertise with a blind tasting at my apartment. Since he was acquainted with members of the Torres family, who are legendary Spanish winemakers, I chose a Torres Grand Coronas for the trial. I uncorked the bottle, poured him a glass in the living room, and left the bottle in a brown paper bag in the kitchen while I went into another room to dress for a dinner date that was to follow.

"Well, what do you think?" I asked him. Brian did all the rituals associated with wine tasting—swirling, sniffing, sipping, chewing, checking for legs, savoring, and began critiquing—"Definitely not California…not French…hmm, smoky, earthy…dusty plum flavor with a hint of pepper…I'd say Spanish…probably from the Penedes region…I'll say a Torres wine…like Gran Coronas."

I was flabbergasted and squeaked in admiration "How did you do that?" Chuckling, Brian said "I looked inside the bag, of course!"

Brian was tapped by *Chronicle Books* to write a biography titled *John Steinbeck: The California Years.* His research and integrity were admirable. He set out to read and immerse himself in every work by Steinbeck before starting his own book. In the days before eBay, Amazon, and Good reads, acquiring rare and out-of-print books was a formidable task. Libraries and used book stores were combed. When Brian's writing was completed, he donated all the materials he had accumulated to the John Steinbeck Library in Salinas, California. He received a thank you note that conveyed special gratitude for the "valuable first edition."

I was a beneficiary of the perks of Brian's job at the Wine Institute: Posh dinners at places like Mondavi vineyards. Cooking demonstrations by celebrity chefs. Wine tastings with the crème of California wine industry luminaries—and, most memorably, meeting the esteemed British writer, Cyril Ray.

The editions of *Punch* that I received every month and shared with Sam, carried, not only Alan Coren's hilarity, but a wine column written by Cyril Ray. However, he was a prolific writer on many topics. In his extraordinary life, Cyril had been war reporter in World War II, foreign correspondent, broadcaster, book reviewer, drama and film critic, and a magazine editor. But, it was wine that brought him to San Francisco in 1984, a swanky shindig held at the Fairmont Hotel to celebrate his latest book, *Robert Mondavi of the Napa Valley*.

Cyril was a diminutive man, who wore round granny glasses. His silver hair was slicked down in the non-style of more serious times. He was magnetic and instantly likeable. And, he was the epitome of everything I loved about the British. We hit it off immediately. I imagine turning strangers into fans within moments was a regular occurrence for Cyril.

Fortunately, I was able to see Cyril again the following year when Brian was in charge of a California wine tasting at the U.S. Embassy in London. Cyril and his wife, Elizabeth, who was a well-known cookbook author, invited us out to dinner and afterwards for more conversation at their apartment in The Albany.

That residence, near Piccadilly Circus, was originally a three-story mansion built in the 1770s, and subdivided into "bachelor" apartments in 1802. The list of notable occupants, who passed through Albany, is dazzling, including writers like Lord Byron, Bulwer-Lytton, Kenneth Clark, Aldous Huxley, and Malcolm Muggeridge.

We all drank brandy while a little fire burned in the gas grate. A question from me about the phrase "Oxford's dreaming spires" prompted Cyril, who attended Oxford, to read from the poetry of Matthew Arnold. The phrase comes from a long, elegiac poem called "Thyrsis." Thankfully, Cyril skipped past that and got to "Dover Beach," which always raises goosebumps. Between the past residents and the present company, it was an Anglophile's dream come true.

Ah, love, let us be true
To one another! for the world, which seems
To lie before us like a land of dreams,
So various, so beautiful, so new,
Hath really, neither joy, nor love, nor light,
Nor certitude, nor peace, nor help for pain;
And we are here as on a darkling plain
Swept with confused alarms of struggle and flight,
Where ignorant armies clash by night...Dover Beach

C. David Burgin was in and out of Bay Area newspaper publishing for many years. He was touted as a "troubleshooter" for failing newspapers, which unfortunately were increasingly common as the news-consuming public turned to other sources. Nevertheless, Burgin, whose bio reflected a lifetime spent in the newspaper business, believed the terminal patients of print could be revived with good writing, colorful features, and the force of personality—his.

Inevitably, Burgin was referred to as a character from *Front Page,* a 1928 Broadway play by Ben Hecht and Charles MacArthur. No one seemed to ask if that dated comparison boded well for the 1980s, which were on the doorstep of the digital age. In 1985, the San Francisco *Examiner,* once the "Monarch of the Dailies" which had long been owned by the Hearst Corporation, hired Burgin for his purported CPR skills.

Burgin's ability to schmooze experienced news' magnates into handing him the reins is remarkable in hindsight. However, he had a repertoire of amusing anecdotes, polished like sea glass, which supported his credentials and personal mythology. If one were paying close attention to his engaging self-promotions, worrisome clues might be detected.

For example, he readily related that a girlfriend had broken up with him. He begged for another chance, saying "I made a mistake." She was unmoved and replied "Mistake? Or character flaw?"

His oft-repeated admission of her appraisal went beyond self-deprecation into the realm of stigmata.

The schmooze worked on William Randolph Hearst III. Burgin's arrival at the *Ex* was heralded with several television commercials, shot in black and white with dramatic lighting, that showed reporters scurrying in fright as Burgin lumbered into view. (Front Page meets film noir.) Among his questionable innovations were installing gonzo journalist, Hunter S. Thompson, as a columnist, and publishing the comic strip *Zippy the Pinhead* inside the paper, not the funnies.

Burgin also gave me the opportunity to write several humor columns for the *Ex,* so I may have been part of his questionable innovations.

In any case, Hearst fired Burgin after only seven months. Ever the peripatetic survivor, Burgin was soon employed again by William

Dean Singleton, a longtime friend, who hired him for double duty in Texas, overseeing the *Dallas Times Herald* and *Houston Post*. As Editor-in-Chief of the *Times Herald*, Burgin flew me to Dallas proffering a columnist job. He invited me to his home for dinner where I met his first wife, who he unfailingly mentioned had won a Pulitzer Prize.

He arranged for several *Times Herald* staffers to take me for a get-acquainted lunch. Breaking bread with people who are seething with rage at what they perceive as an outsider taking a position they covet, is not good for camaraderie—or the digestion.

On my own, I explored a bit, having high tea at a venerable downtown Dallas hotel and bought a ticket to ride the elevator to the top of the Reunion Tower. Burgin laughingly responded "You paid to go up the Tower? Hell, you can stand on a beer can and see for a hundred miles!"

Could I trade the cool, fog-wreathed charms of San Francisco for the hundred-mile views and heat of Texas? The offer was tempting. Texans are a unique breed, colorful, out-spoken, and independent. The Dallas-Fort Worth area offered big city sophistication and cowboy heritage. I might finally have indulged a fascination with horses and riding I'd had since childhood.

On the other hand, I was probably too inexperienced at that point. I'd have been in an unfamiliar city in a newsroom of malcontent colleagues where political correctness was beginning to infect journalism. And, I'd have been under the control of Burgin, who, behind the jokes and jovial retelling of familiar tales, might be a tyrant.

That was exactly the position I would find myself in a few years later. But, that's another story.

10
Power Brokers, Politicians, & Rat Wrangling

Remember the Power lunch? Three martinis, hearts of romaine drenched in Roquefort dressing, blood-seeping sirloin steaks, thin cut *pomme frites*, brandy and cigars afterwards? If it still existed in pockets of paleo-corporate diehards, the vegan, Starbucks, younger generation, put the Power Lunch on life support, and the 2021 pandemic lockdown and Zoom meetings killed it.

However, in the 1980s, the Power Lunch, with an Italian twist at WSB&G, was particularly attractive to the San Francisco City Hall types. The din of conversation, clatter of cutlery, clinking of glasses, rattling of bar dice and flops on the bar counter, raucous laughter, and shouted greetings across a crowded room, ramped up the energy.

The Power Lunch, more than any other feature, probably defined WSB&G in the public mind, thanks to the local media, which was always speculating about the goings-on at Bohemian Grove, corporate boardrooms, and Alpha Male poker games, where secret deals were made. That information was much harder to glean in the days before leaked emails and hacked personal accounts. Without any specifics to go on, the print media constantly assured readers that big stuff and deals made-on-a-handshake were going on five days a week at WSB&G.

Craziness at noon was not my preference. Years of working in the evening had turned me into a night owl with an internal clock that was set to rise late, attend classes, serve food at dinner time, enjoy after-work camaraderie, rinse, lather, repeat. I imagine most wait staffers also enjoy dependable hours and expectation of uninterrupted life outside of work where they can pursue their interests or care for their families.

However, most restaurant employers demand food servers be available for all shifts, weekends, and overtime. That always struck me as an insult to individual dignity. Who wants to surrender the autonomy to schedule doctors' appointments, children's activities, and myriad weekly activities just to collect a paycheck from a boss who considers you a Lego block? Sometimes a newbie had no choice.

That was the case with Bobby Ryder, who was raising a young son on his own. Bobby was a thin, tiny man with a craggy face and a super-sized sense of humor, who was a great favorite with staff and customers. Self-deprecating about his diminutive size, Bobby joked that he used to be a bouncer at a daycare center.

As the newest member of the staff and with no set schedule, Bobby was the utility man, filling in for waiters taking sick days or vacations. He was constantly in demand and probably worked more shifts, day and night, than anyone else. But, arranging babysitters for his child must have been a nightmare.

Bobby was often working unfamiliar *stations*. Having a regular station enhances a food server's efficiency. Ideally, they can see all their tables in a glance, bundle together several tasks, so as to maximize every trip to the kitchen or the service bar. Round of drinks for one table, more coffee on another, present the bill at a third—the logistics were fun. Familiarity with a regular station results in economy of motion. The Union seniority rules allowed for servers to choose the station they wanted, but some people were happy where they were.

I was taking classes in commercial illustration at the San Francisco Art Academy, so keeping my days free to attend, plus my aversion to the manic pace of the lunch shift, made me a target for Ed. Incoming Dodge Ball! He decreed that I also work during the day. That didn't last long, but afforded me a hilarious Ed incident involving Mayor Dianne Feinstein.

When I started at WSB&G, George Moscone was the mayor of San Francisco and Feinstein was President of the Board of Supervisors. Moscone, who was called "the people's mayor," liked to get out and about in the evening, and was a cheerful, expansive figure when he had drinks at Washington Square Bar & Grill. Moscone's assassination in 1978 by Dan White was an enormous shock to the City, as was White's despicable murder of Supervisor Harvey Milk.

Overnight, the tragedy elevated Feinstein to the office of Mayor. I served Feinstein and her third husband, Richard Blum, a couple times during my lunch purgatory. She was a polite and pleasant person. But, on one occasion, I overheard a dispute she was having with Blum. She was going to order Fettucine Chef Bardelli, which was an alfredo sauce with shallots, mushrooms, and a splash of marinara. Blum wanted to share it with her. Feinstein was hissing at him *sotto voce,* as married couples do, "Dick, I want my own order."

To understand what follows, I must note that Mary Etta Moose had ongoing problems with her weight. Given how autocratic Ed was about almost everything, I can imagine he also intruded himself into Mary Etta's diet programs. Sovereignty over one's own body should be a private matter, but Ed could be oblivious to boundaries, especially when he was bedazzled by the presence of celebrities.

Ed was hovering nearby when I placed a full order of Fettucine Bardelli in front of the Mayor, who had won the argument with her husband about what and how much she wanted. She draped her napkin across her lap and picked up her cutlery in anticipation of a delicious meal. Suddenly, Ed swooped in, picked up the plate, and said "Oh, Mayor, you don't want all that."

He returned with a mini plate of pasta and placed it in front of the mayor. The looks on the faces of Feinstein and Blum were priceless.

Mayor Feinstein became so exasperated with the relentless criticism of journalist Warren Hinckle that she poured a drink over him at a public event. Hinckle was a born and raised San Francisco, Irish, Catholic, character who rose to prominence in the 1960s when he transformed *Ramparts* magazine from a sedate Catholic quarterly into a muck-raking, anti-war, bullhorn for the radical Left.

As he bounced from one editing gig to another, Hinckle's extravagance and self-promotion left craters where publications used to be. His writing abilities were legendary and he was said to dictate his newspaper columns for the *Chronicle* and *Examiner* from barstools right up against deadlines.

In short, Hinckle was the kind of flamboyant, warts-and-all, character the City loved. He had raised eccentric to an art form. His long, straight hair was held in place by the strap of a black eye patch covering the socket of an eye lost in a childhood accident. By the 1980s, he was becoming corpulent. His skin was the pink-ish color of a fresh cut pork chop. His distinctive, gravelly voice could dominate, not just a conversation, but an entire room.

His constant companion was a Basset Hound named Bentley, who managed to adapt its suitcase-shaped body into any number of barroom crevices. It was that sort of scenario, Bentley tucked under a chair and Hinckle holding forth, when I reached over his shoulder to serve him another Screwdriver. Hinckle gesticulated wildly to make a point. The drink tumbled mid-air and soaked the front of his shirt. Perhaps, his previous baptism by Mayor Feinstein accounts for his composure. Without interrupting his spiel, he mopped the front of his shirt with a napkin, and interjected several times, "It's okay, It's okay."

Dave Jenkins was a frequent lunch presence and the bane of maître d's trying to work out seating arrangements. Jenkins was a former longshoreman, who became a powerful figure in the City's labor movement. He was a big, heavy, fellow with a florid complexion, wispy white hairs sprouting from his scalp, and eyes twinkling with mischief. However, when Jenkins hefted himself through the front door, like a freighter plowing through heavy swells under the Golden Gate, he would take the first available berth, generally a prized window table that had been promised to someone on the waiting list. No tugboat or frustrated host was going to move him.

Jenkins' jolly personality made up for the inconvenience. Everyone, from food servers to politicians, would stop by his table for Dave's raspy-voiced benedictions. His daughter told me they had once been stuck in a huge traffic jam, but Dave rolled down the car window, and soon had the frustrated motorists involved in a comical, multi-car conversation.

While the frantic pace of the Power Lunch shifts was off putting, I was also uncomfortable with the sharp elbow atmosphere. Everyone was trying to get business done, get noticed, get ahead, get connected, or faking all the foregoing. The City was so special that most people desperately wanted to be special too, to find a way, even if it meant riding rough-shod over others, to appear in the firmament of notables. The noise, the posturing, aggression, and pretense could be overwhelming.

For quite a few, a longtime connection to the City was sufficient to establish their specialness. Thus, they would announce themselves as "fourth generation San Franciscan and fifth generation Californian." It was a constant refrain that immediately followed an introduction. I called them the Fourth and Fifth People. That pedigree might be a stand-alone that didn't need to be attached to any actual accomplishments.

Such was the case with High Horse Harry, who was so besotted with his City and California roots that he had become pot bound. He had nothing to offer conversationally other than unsolicited advice derived from the accident of his birth. He had no concept of None of Your Business. He would button hole me while I was working to give instructions on what was and wasn't acceptable in San Francisco. The view from a high horse was supposed to be 20/20.

When I added blonde highlights to my brown hair and eventually went all blonde, Harry predicted disaster. "That's just not done in San Francisco." Actually, it worked out just fine. In fact, every woman might want to be blonde at some point in life.

The cumulative effect of the Fourth and Fifth People was to suggest newcomers would never really be accepted. At the same time that San Francisco was a world class city in many ways, there was an element of provincialism and strong whiff of elitism. I imagine the Fourth and Fifths gave birth to a generation of "Fifth and Sixth People" that have governed the City into its current condition. I wish I could go back in time and whisper two words into Harry's ear—hybrid vigor.

While the Power Lunch was popular with City Hall types, it brought them in contact with The People they claimed to represent, and therein was a contradiction. With the exception of Mayor Feinstein, I found the local pols were usually uncivil, arrogant, distant, and cheap. Among the churlish Champions of The Downtrodden, U.S. Rep. Phillip Burton was a stand out. Nothing said "You are an Invisible Prole" like being summoned to his table to take an order and made to stand there until Burton was damn good and ready to interrupt his discussions of great affairs of state to grunt out his lunch selection. *Yo, Congressman, your huddled masses, right here, yearning to hear what you want to eat.*

In the evenings, the state politicians were likely to turn up. I served California Lieutenant Governor Leo McCarthy and five companions. The meal went without incident, everyone seemed happy, and McCarthy presented his credit card for the bill, which was $150, pretty inexpensive for six people. I put the card through the technology of the time, which was a motorized machine that ran a carbon receipt over the raised information on the card and produced three copies.

McCarthy signed the receipt, entered an amount on the tip line, and handed it back to me to total. He had entered 16—. That was a bit light at a time when many people were tipping 20%.

But, I never made a fuss about chintzy tips because many people over tip and it evens out. I totaled the bill as $166.00.

However, McCarthy blew up. He said the six was actually a zero and I was trying to cheat him. It was humiliating and kinda felt like a setup. (Not that a politician would ever be shady.) Apparently, his guests also felt something was amiss. One of them came back afterwards and gave me a twenty-dollar bill.

Being accused of thievery is an occupational hazard in the restaurant business. Like many servers, I've turned in countless cameras, sunglasses, wallets, phones, clothing (even dentures!) to the Lost and Found. But, thievery does occur. Stereotypes don't persist without being refreshed.

A woman wearing a large, gold-link bracelet dined with her husband and another couple. They were all convivial and fun to serve. At the end of the meal, the woman suddenly accused me, furiously, of stealing the expensive bracelet. Indeed, her wrist was bare. How could I manage to steal it off her wrist in front of three other people? She was enraged when they left, and I wondered "Am I going to be charged with a crime?"

An hour later, the woman returned and showed me the bracelet, lying around her ankle inside her pantyhose. She had used the toilet in the ladies' room, lowered the pantyhose, and the golden bracelet dropped into the nylons. She was deeply apologetic and embarrassed. I was impressed at the innate good character of a person, who would own up to a situation and admit to a mistake. Apologies were not uncommon in those days. Now, there's been a hardening of ego such that even the word "Oops" is rarely heard.

Fire Chief Andrew Casper, who had been appointed by Mayor Moscone, served from 1976-82. Firefighters are particularly revered in a San Francisco because of its combustible history. The 1906 earthquake that initiated a massive fire is, perhaps, the most well-known, but the City has always been vulnerable to fire. Many wooden structures remained. Andy was an occasional and very congenial customer at WSB&G. It was always nice to see him. One week, I saw him twice on the block where I lived, supervising a second fire on the third floor of the same building. He recognized me and motioned for me to step over the hoses to join him. To quell my concerns, Andy explained a malcontent kid was setting fires in his family's dwelling, which wasn't too quelling.

Willie Brown, as Speaker of the Assembly, was one of the most powerful figures in Californian politics. He, Herb Caen, and society haberdasher, Wilkes Bashford, a seemingly odd triumvirate, supposedly had lunch together every day at Le Central on Bush Street, conveniently located near Bashford's store on Union Square. Brown and Caen showed up together in my station one evening, and Brown kicked off the proceedings by leering at me and muttering something on the order of "Oh, baby." His casual lechery came across as standard operating procedure. Did any women find it charming? It was unwelcome—and ridiculous. A scroungy tomcat in a Brioni suit, I thought.

The two men, side by side, were a contrast in how to wield power. Brown was a wheeler-dealer and arm twister whose lengthy political record was tarnished by accusations of cronyism and pay-to-play. And, the scroungy tomcat thing.

Herb, who wielded power of a different sort, was always a gentleman, reserved, even a bit subdued in demeanor. Accusations were thrown about that Herb's reviews were for sale and that his meals were always *comped* by restaurant owners. I never saw any of that. The slurs, I believe, came from those, who were envious of Herb's exalted position, which had been arrived at through years of work and talent. Envy is one of the seven deadly sins, the most insidious I feel, because it often masquerades as virtue.

Jesse Hamlin, a *Chronicle* writer, was Herb Caen's assistant for six years. In a 2009 article, he described the phenomenon of the man and his literary place in the City this way:

"The Column, capital C, was a monolith made of malleable bits and pieces—a marvelous democratic jumble where Danielle Steel might share space with Sister Boom Boom, the satiric transvestite, and a good line from a panhandler got the same play as a statesman's bon mot. Herb's joy and burden was to fill that monolith day after day. He did it with a singular mix of creativity and discipline. He constantly cooked up zingers and word games, verbal riffs and poetic images, yet he went about his business with the meticulousness of a banker."

Herb and Hamlin's day began promptly at 9:30 a.m. when they considered the letters and phone calls that arrived overnight, then melded those with snippets, gossip, and morsels, they'd sniffed out themselves. At 11:30, Herb began typing with two fingers on his Royal standard typewriter, a piece of equipment that was antiquated even then. The resultant 1000-word column was overlaid on a mockup pattern to assure it would fit the allotted space in the paper. Adjustments were made and Herb, who lived by "Brevity is the soul of wit" found ways to abbreviate brevity. After writing thank you notes to readers who'd submitted items, Herb was out the door by 1 p.m. to begin rounding up material for the next day's column. And, he did that for nearly 60 years.

When I began to get a little recognition for my writing, some of the City Hall types deigned to speak to me as a vaguely human entity, while still treating my co-workers like subservient drones. If that was meant to endear the Champions of the People to me, it failed. Hypocrisy added to elitism is a lateral move.

There was a small category of customers I called "wall birds." The service bar was situated next to the men's room, adjacent to one entrance to the kitchen, and a blank wall provided standing-room-only for visitors, who just wanted a drink and a chance to chat up their favorite staff members. KRON reporter, Karl Sonkin, stopped by frequently. Another wall bird was Clint Reilly, a political consultant and campaign manager dubbed "The Kingmaker," who helped launch the careers of Dianne Feinstein, Nancy Pelosi, Barbara Boxer, and many more. Clint was a former seminarian, a teetotaler, and a deeply serious guy. My interest in politics didn't develop until much later, but I never forgot something Clint said, which was "Good people don't go into politics anymore."

The Democrat Convention of 1984, which produced the Mondale/Ferraro ticket, was also a hot ticket for the Washington Square Bar & Grill. Political types, media figures, and TV broadcasters flocked to the City's most famous saloon. Write ups in local and national publications brought hordes of on-lookers. I was serving Robin McNeil of the *McNeil-Lehrer Report* and looked over my shoulder to see gawkers standing three-deep outside the windows.

There was an oft-told tale about an individual, who was trying to get through the throng on the sidewalk and was insistent about being allowed inside. The crowd may have been resentful the individual got preferential treatment. But, it was Ed Moose.

Sofi recalls an episode when Walter Mondale was dining at WSB&G and his Secret Service guys were in the kitchen to monitor the preparation of his food. As the junior chef, Edgar often had to be the Rodent Wrangler. (Mice and rats found many nooks and crannies in the decrepit city block that housed WSB&G, and sought the delicious morsels that hit the floor.) Edgar hated vermin duty, but had become quite good at it.

While the Secret Service guys supervised the meal prep, Edgar was wielding a couple sauté pans—when a rat popped up by the stove. Without missing a beat, he stomped the creature and kept on cooking. The agents were impressed and said "That's the kind of guy we need!"

With the exception of Dan Rather, who seemed to play the coy virgin by staying away from WSB&G during the Convention, all the Media Big Wigs showed up for lunch or dinner or both. Sightings included: Walter Cronkite, David Brinkley, Peter Jennings, Sam Donaldson, Mike Royko, Studs Terkel, and George Will.

Ed was in heaven. Even Sam's imperturbable cool gave way to mildly giddy enthusiasm. My favorite recollection involved Tom Brokaw.

Over many years of waiting tables, I was the-fly-on-the-wall, the unacknowledged fifth wheel, the interpreter of conversational fragments, and the silent witness to many customer interactions. I became proficient at reading body language and sniffing pheromones wafted into the air. I often detected which regulars were attracted to each other and would, several weeks later, become couples.

Thus, I noticed a situation brewing with Tom Brokaw. At that time, he was the anchor of *NBC Nightly News* and his speech irregularity, called a Liquid L, was familiar to viewers and satirized by some comedians. The Liquid L sounds like a gulping sound in words where L occurs, but didn't hinder Brokaw from a hugely successful career.

One evening during the convention, I saw Brokaw locking eyes with a gorgeous young woman at a nearby table. Communication, on the beautiful-powerful-people-frequency, seemed to fly between them. At the same moment, eyes still locked, they both rose slowly from their chairs and drifted toward the door. Of course, I could be wrong, but it appeared Brokaw was going to get luh-lucky.

While the Democrat Convention meant gang-busters' business and publicity for WSB&G, the rest of the City didn't share the wealth. For two years, the restaurant and hospitality industries had geared up for, what it believed, would be a bonanza—that turned out to be a bust. Restaurants stood empty. Retail stores and tourist attractions actually saw business fall off. Even traffic in and out of the City dropped noticeably. Many explanations were offered for the disappointment, including the plethora of private parties that laid on food and drink freebies. The forecasters, who anticipated the convention-to-end-all conventions, failed to consider that politicians, when they can't spend other peoples' money, don't spend their own.

Once again, Ed saw the promotional possibilities in the gathering of celebrities that were attending the Democrat Convention. He organized a softball game where it all started, on the North Beach playground, between his Lapins Sauvages and mixed team of media and politicians.

Ron Fimrite, the softball poet laureate, who could always provide play-by-play coverage, reported that the media team included Tom Brokaw, Bryant Gumbel, Peter Jennings, Jeff Greenfield, and New York Governor, Mario Cuomo, who opted for a bipartisan, fence-straddling move that didn't work out too well.

Fimrite wrote, "Cuomo, the convention's key note speaker, actually played for both sides, grounding out for the media side and singling a home run for the winning Lapins side."

Nowadays, it's hard to imagine such a casual, egalitarian gathering of mega-stars, wanna be jocks, guys from the neighborhood, camp followers, and curious passersby, assembling for an unseasonable softball game in November on a time-worn ball field tucked into an eccentric neighborhood. But that was then.

San Francisco in the 1980s was unconstrained by intrusive paparazzi, crazed fans with mental issues and guns, shouting protestors with signs, and flash mobs quickly called forth by social media to shut down anything they disagree with. At that time, fun could break out and be safely engaged in. Memories could be stored up for a lifetime. I miss those days.

11

Fandom, Forks, & Food Serving Units

In the 1970s, a college professor I dated briefly gave me a biography of Lady Ottoline Morrell that was to shape my reading habits for years. Lady Ottoline was an English aristocrat, who was a patron of struggling writers and painters, and created a salon where intellectuals of her time could meet. She was also a randy old gal. The list of her affairs is long, celebrity-rich, and included many members of the Bloomsbury Group, which took its name from a district in London's West End. The most famous member of the assemblage that Americans would know, is Virginia Woolf.

I became fascinated with the Bloomsbury Group, which was LGBTQ long before that had an alphabet label and whose sexual hijinks were the equal of anything now. Without the luxury of ordering online, I gathered quite a library of Bloomsbury biographies, many obtained from rare bookstores on trips to London. No one else shared that interest and it was a solitary and impractical pleasure until I met Robert Hughes. That is, if 30 seconds can be considered a meeting.

Australian born Robert Hughes, was a painter, art critic, and prolific author on numerous topics, who became the art critic for *Time* magazine where I became a fan of his brilliant writing. Hughes was also ruggedly handsome, rode a motorcycle, and ran counter to an image of art critics as pencil neck, asexual academics.

In 1980, the BBC presented *The Shock of the New,* a multi-part series on modern art based on Hughes' book of the same name. When his book tour came to a San Francisco bookstore, I waited in the autograph line with his five-pound book clutched to my chest, palms sweating, heart fluttering.

As I approached his eminence, I realized he, and he alone, could answer an allegation that arose from my Bloomsbury Group reading: That Roger Fry, one of the most influential art critics of his time, purposely ruined the career of painter, Wyndham Lewis, whose work I admired. If a personal vendetta could wreck a career then, perhaps it still could, so I was interested.

I placed my copy in front of Robert Hughes. Pen in hand, he opened to the title page and I popped the question, "Did Roger Fry ruin Wyndham Lewis's career?" He paused (Shock of the New Unexpected Question) leaned back in his chair, and warmed to the subject.

"Yes, indeed, he did," and Lewis's work had been unfairly overlooked as a result, he said, then prepared to say more. About that time, a book store commissar standing nearby, coughed as a reminder we were at a time-sensitive, profit-seeking venture not an Ottoline Morrell soiree.

Were years of private study vindicated by a brief exchange with Robert Hughes? For me the question, then and now, has to do with knowledge for its own sake. Or an interest that's nurtured with no apparent application. Is it worthwhile or a waste of gray cell space? Turns out the answer is fickle.

Who could have imagined that two guys with knowledge of rusty signs, outdated toys, and discarded promotional items, could put that information to use—profitably? Yet, Mike Wolfe and Frank Fritz starred in the successful TV show *American Pickers*. Similarly, survivalists and modern-day hunter-gatherers in Alaska are paid to display their knowledge on TV shows like *Life Below Zero* for audiences with freezers full of Ben & Jerry's ice cream and where Siri sets the temperature.

Those examples may give hope to recent college graduates, who are staggering under the weight of student loan debt, with degrees in Gender studies or French literature, that a career windfall might await them. Having also traveled the learn-what-you-love route, I offer this advice: Follow what intrigues you, but develop a hands-on skill that other people need. If I had a do-over, I'd major in English Lit, and minor in welding. Instead, I chose waitressing.

A waitress, whether a carhop on roller skates or a hash slinger in a diner, a waiter in a tuxedo performing a tableside preparation of Crepes Suzettes *en flambe,* are all food-serving units. The work of food-serving units can be drudgery or fulfilling depending on one's personality and what the work environment affords. Washington Square Bar & Grill allowed all kinds of food-serving units to explore the intersections between their personalities and customers.

Sofi Kurtz was so imbued with her Ivy League training as a psychiatric social worker, she couldn't turn it off. Her tableside manner combined wisecracks with genuinely insightful observations. However, she was awestruck when finding James Earl Jones at one of her tables. His *basso profundo* voice had enriched film, stage, and voice over, performances for decades. Sofi acknowledged her respect in typical Sofi fashion:

Sofi: Mr. Jones, I have a request.
Jones: What is it?
Sofi: Would you read the menu aloud?

Bobby Ryder was an outrageous showman. He might approach a table and mimic a magician, who jerks the tablecloth out from under the plates. Or relate the latest chapter of his lovelorn dating life. He developed a following of regulars, who wanted a side of madcap with their dining experience.

Marcy Campagne was a firecracker of exuberance. Her laughter was constantly triggered and resounded through the dining room. Few sounds are as infectious as spontaneous laughter. Her customers caught the bug and the rest of us enjoyed the background cackle.

For me, each table of new customers was a culinary blind date. What did they expect from the famous saloon? How could I facilitate a good experience? And what was their relationship with food? The act of eating is fraught with tension and emotion. After all, it's our first primal experience. We exit from a warm uterus soup. We are up-ended by the ankles and given a jump-start smack on the buttocks. Then, it's time to eat.

Every day thereafter, we must eat. How much? How little? Who provides it? Where does it come from? Under what circumstances? The father of my dearest friend was a self-important, verbally abusive, bully, who used the dinner table as a forum for expressing disappointment in his family's shortcomings. For the rest of my friend's life that uncomfortable association with food was visible in the anxiety of her body language. She held a fork in her right hand, but the fingers of her left hand were tightly curled around her thumb. I had no trouble imagining who that fist was for.

Sidebar:

Male customer: What's the soup du jour?
Me: Cream of asparagus.

Male customer: That's so feminine. Do you have anything else?
Me: How about the cream of leather?

Treating each table like a blind date, could have surprising out-comes. An atypical couple arrived in my station at 6 p.m. on a Tuesday evening. Termed *early birds* by other waiters, they were not fashionably dressed, would order from the cheaper items, and might, if overcome with a wild notion, order a glass of house wine with dinner. The vibe was pastor and wife from the outer 'burbs checking out the famous saloon they'd read about in Herb Caen's column. At that time of day, early in the week, nothing was going to connect them to the magic of WSB&G. But, I could try.

With no other customers to distract me, I had time to explain the Italian items on the menu, relate the cuisine to the inhabitants of North Beach, and tell a few tales of kooks and celebrities, who'd enlivened the place. They were amused, entertained, and felt what we all want—included. As they prepared to leave, the lady took my hand, gave it a warm squeeze, and said, "Amazing grace."

The remark astonished me—until I recalled the gist of the old hymn is a wretch in need of saving.

The value of loyal, engaging, food-serving units seemed to fade with Ed Moose as the decade went on. When I was first hired, there were a few flat-out, drugged-out, boozy wackos that were eventually replaced by a reliable crew of vibrant but competent staffers, who were foundational in part to WSB&G's reputation. [Writer Kevin Garcia wrote "The saloon became home to some of the best barmen, waitresses, and hosts the City has seen…"]

An atmosphere of warmth and welcome was conveyed by the staff to customers old and new. For regulars, WSB&G felt like a club, but newcomers were not made to feel that it was a private club. There was enough fun to go around; new clubs and friendships could be formed.

Of course, Ed Moose was a genius at getting high profile people in the door, but keeping them there and coming back were functions affably performed by food-serving units and drink-serving units. The collective contributions of a good team seemed to be less appreciated by Ed as, increasingly, ambition seemed to goad him. How much attention could he derive from being the City's most famous bar owner? He was Macbeth, bound within the biscotti box that was trying to be a restaurant. As his press clippings accumulated, his do-gooder side diminished. He seemed less willing to share credit or the spotlight with others.

A preference for new staff members, who were of lower wattage, crept in. WSB&G once sought to be the West Coast version of New York's Artist and Writers restaurant. Ed said one of the secrets to the saloon's success was hiring "[B]right, sophisticated people who know about theater and music…" But, the tone began to change. Increasingly, those staffers Ed conferred his favor upon were not the lively, clever types associated with WSB&G's earlier days.

Leading the changes was Mark Schachern, a former teacher, who had supplemented his income by working in the bar business. Mark was from Detroit and his father had been in the newspaper business, a connection that always triggered the ex-newsie in Ed. Moreover, Mark was a fairly good softball player, although his age and liver condition didn't comport with Ed's requirements. Mark was originally hired at WSB&G as a waiter, could stand in as a bartender, but in relatively short order and inexplicably, was elevated to a "partner." The staff was astonished by the partner announcement. Mark was an amiable guy, rather diffident in manner, but didn't seem particularly noteworthy.

What purpose would he serve? Ed was the front-of-the-house personality. Mary Etta was the food supervisor. Sam was the nuts-and-bolts engineer. Mark didn't seem to have the sparkle to shine in that stellar firmament. And, there were no plans for the bosses to step back from their responsibilities. Everyone else in the operation performed their jobs well and didn't need instruction from a newbie. What would Mark do?

Around that time, I believe, Ed began referring to himself as the CEO of WSB&G, so Mark may have been a prop to Ed's grandiosity. Supposedly, Mark was to be in charge of hiring, firing, and admonishing misbehavior. Inevitably, some attrition of the core staffers occurred. Life goes on and even the best job ever must be left behind. So, that gave Mark opportunities.

The new hires, as chosen by Mark, were meant to change the tone of WSB&G. The term for this was "more professional." The saloon was doing record business and the kind of staff, which helped achieve that was inexplicably deemed not professional enough. In practice, Mark's hires moved the staff from animated to animatronic. Certainly not "[B]right, sophisticated people who could talk about theater and music…"

One of the new hires announced piously that he didn't sing "Happy Birthday" to customers. Corny? Yeah. But, most people spend their whole lives without feeling special. A little recognition on their birthdays doesn't seem like a hardship. Especially if it could be spiced up with staff quirkiness. And, making customers feel special had been a hallmark of the old staff.

In the new hiring practices, male food-serving units were preferred by Ed and Mark. Many of them had been fired from Perry's. How is being sacked a resume enhancement? Perry's on Union Street was the only saloon that came close to the popularity of WSB&G in those days. While its Irish bartenders were legendary and the bar side lively, I found the food service cool and distant. The waiters were impersonal and gave off a kind of frat boy vibe one would experience as an unwelcome guest at Sigma Nu.

One of the ex-Perry hires brought into WSB&G, wouldn't even make eye contact and was so devoid of personality, I thought he might have a circuit board under his collar. That was deemed the kind of staff WSB&G needed as Mark was put in charge of recruiting more *professional* help. Kevin Clancy was Perry graduate and an epic fail of the new hiring practices.

Kevin was a beautiful young man with fair skin, dark hair, and blue eyes, who was wired like a pipe bomb. When his longtime girlfriend broke up with him, Kevin seemed to burst from any restraints to his volatile temperament. At best, he had a sizzling energy; at worst, his fists did the talking. He was hired as a maître d. That is, the first point of contact for customers. One evening, he had a disagreement with someone that he settled with a beatdown on the sidewalk in front of WSB&G.

The fisticuffs incident saved my job. A doyenne of the Nob Hill set, whose face I recognized from the society pages, arrived with a companion at 5 pm, an hour before the restaurant opened for dinner. Ed had decreed that service must not begin before 6 pm in consideration of the many tasks that occupied the cooks. I explained that to the society woman, who began stamping her alligator footwear, and demanding to be served. When I continued to refuse, she left in a huff.

The problem with people, who want to be served well in advance of opening, is like the camel getting its nose under the tent. They beg for a crust of bread or a cup of gruel, but once seated, they forget they agreed to a bowl of soup. Instead, they order a steak sandwich, Caesar salad prepared tableside, and hot apple pie with hand-cranked ice cream.

Since the society lady might complain to Ed, I thought it best to report the incident. I believed I detected a gleam in Ed's eye as he thought I'd finally committed a fire-able offense. Clearly, he was building up to that, huffing and puffing about the seriousness of the affront. Never mind that I was just following his directive about no meal service before 6.

That's when I noted to Ed that, ahem, I hadn't taken her out to the sidewalk for a round of cat fighting and hair-pulling. Or words to that effect, which clearly were a Kevin reference. Ed was still capable at that point of recognizing a double standard. Once again, I escaped the pink slip.

Sam never seemed to lose his appreciation of eccentric staffers and their talents. A child of wealth, comfortable for life, Sam was, nevertheless, a reliable supporter of the proletariat. Pianist Mike Greensill recalled a drunk customer, who got hostile when he refused to play "New York, New York," and complained to Sam. Greensill thought he might get sacked. Instead, the grump was thrown out. Sam patted Mike on the back reassuringly and said "If anyone ever gives you trouble, let me know."

Ed's disrespect for, what should have been, valued employees was evident when he dissed Cyril Boyce. Acknowledged as one of the City's best bartenders, Cyril, who was the bar manager, took offense when Ed told him to fix something that was amiss in the men's bathroom. (Generally speaking, telling someone, who is not a plumber, to fix the crapper is uncouth.)

Furthermore, the *facilities* in WSB&G were so cramped, ancient, and decrepit, *something amiss* could mean the floor might have been damaged in the 1906 earthquake and finally collapsed. Or a harbor seal from Fisherman's Wharf had made its way through the drain pipes and poked its head up in the commode.

In any case, it was not Cyril's job and he said so. Apparently, Ed thought he had a *Caine Mutiny* situation on his hands and responded in Captain Queeg fashion. He ordered Cyril to fix the john problem. (Once more unto the breach—and bring a plunger!)

The incident likely was the final item on a list of Ed's autocratic commands that put Cyril over the top. Ed was imperious in ordering his drinks from bartenders, who might be busy serving other people aka customers. And, he would stand behind the bar, obliviously to bartenders trying to assemble drinks while he was plunked in their way. As one of the bartenders during the day, when Ed's posturing for the public was at flood stage, Cyril probably had enough. He removed his bartender apron, tossed it on the bar, and walked out, never to return.

Prior to the Cyril incident, Hal Thunes had a similar experience. He was tending bar when Ed came behind the bar to converse with someone across the plank. After shuffling around Ed's bulk several times, Hal asked the boss if he could move. Ed replied furiously that he was the owner and would stand any damn place he wanted. Hal dropped his apron and walked out. In that case, Ed followed and apologized—but didn't change his behavior.

When Hal eventually quit, his replacements at the front door were bland table-fillers, except for Harry Denton. Raucous, rotund, rascally, and gay, Harry was on a mission to meet everyone and learn everything in preparation for opening Harry's Bar, the first of many ventures. As such, he was just passing through, but left laughter and lots of new friends in his wake. After Hal and Harry, the D in maître d' stood for dull.

Marcy recalls when actor and comedian, Bill Murray, came into WSB&G with several friends and asked for a table where they could have cocktails. Marcy relayed the request to the dullard of the day, who refused.

"It's Billy Murray!" said Marcy. Nope, said the dullard. She apologized to Murray, who took being turned down in good humor. He said to his friends, "Let's go guys, we're too ugly for this place."

My interest in food-serving units and the restaurant business led me on a quirky pilgrimage that was prompted by *I, Claudius*.

The 13-part mini-series on *Masterpiece Theater* about the Roman Emperor, who reigned from 27 BC to 14 AD, was must-watch TV for me. The VCR was just becoming affordable in the late 1970s, but on Sunday evenings at 9 p.m. I was parked in front of my TV. I was taken aback at the final scene of the final episode of *I, Claudius* in which his wicked wife, Agrippina, offers Claudius a poisoned mushroom—on a fork. That seemed historically inaccurate.

The evolution of eating utensils is long and fascinating. Hands, no doubt unwashed, came first. Hollowed out bread called *trenchers* were used by early elites at messy feasts. (Handy to have one's dog under the table to tidy up the overflow.) However, forks made of bone, dating to 2400-1900 BC, have been found in China, but like most early forks, were used for cooking and serving. The concept of a fork for personal use took longer to develop, appearing in the Byzantine Empire in the 4th century. (So, I may have been right about the I, Claudius incident.)

In the 11th century, Italians took up the personal fork. They invented the three-tine fork to more efficiently eat pasta. Some of the Italian swells in the 14th century began carrying their own spoons and forks in special boxes. One can only imagine what petri dishes the fork boxes were.

The rest of Europe was slow to adopt the personal fork, viewing the Italians as fey and foppish. That made French king, Henry IV, interesting. He was king of France from 1589 to 1610. In order to ascend to the throne, he had to convert from the Protestant faith to Catholicism, a decision he struggled with. Finally, he said "Paris is well worth a mass." Goodbye, Luther. Hello, Pope.

Henry seems to have been progressive in matters of eating. He patronized La Tour d' Argent, which was founded in 1582, and is credited as the oldest restaurant in Paris. For much of history, royalty didn't dine out. Inns with limited offerings for travelers and the lower classes preceded restaurants. So why would royalty choose mystery meat stew at an inn when the king's kitchen might be serving roasted, stuffed peacock? Not to the mention the need for the king's taster, who was the first line of defense against poisoning. Yet, Henry dined out.

Despite scorn for the fork elsewhere, Henry popularized the implement with French nobility. On one of the upper floors of La Tour d' Argent, there's a small museum where Henry's personal fork is enshrined. On a trip to Paris, I went to see it. (Let others visit the Eiffel Tower, I'm going to see the fork!) It has a rather menacing appearance. Size-wise it's more like the fork in a carving set, but with flourishes of the early metal workers' art. That protype evolved into myriad forks for specialized uses, such that diners now worry about using the wrong fork.

Thus, the history of eating and restaurants is rich with information both amusing and serious, which were interesting to me as I observed the process day to day. However, I had to attend to the changes at WSB&G that began to reflect creeping misogyny. Increasingly, the new hires were exclusively young men, who wanted to learn the bar business from Ed, the famous publican, and they stood at attention in his presence like Labrador puppies anticipating thrown tennis balls.

As Mark was supposedly the talent agent, culling Perry rejects to hire new, sycophantic staffers, I felt he was changing part of the essential nature of WSB&G. A job at the famous saloon was a plum and shouldn't be given to those, who added nothing to the mix. Yet, that was the new direction.

One exception was Jan Schachern, Mark's wife, who worked as a WSB&G waitress for a time. She was a cheerful, fresh-faced, natural blonde, who'd attended college at Ohio Wesleyan where she took theater classes. She still carried a wholesome Midwest quality and was very generous with her connections. During my singing phase, she introduced me to her friend Paul Rogers, who was a composer and pianist and we recorded a demo tape in his studio.

When Jan acquired two tickets to an extraordinary event at Zellerbach Hall in Berkeley, she invited me to see (gasp!) Rudolf Nureyev with the Dutch National Ballet. During the San Francisco ballet season, I would usually buy a ticket for, at least, one ballet, the kind of ticket that put my seat closer to Daly City than the stage. At the Nureyev event, we were seated about three rows from the orchestra pit and had a closeup view of the greatest dancer of the 20th century.

Nureyev danced a solo from *Le Corsaire* as well as selections with other dancers. What struck me from that close vantage point was the effort of ballet expressed in squeaking toe shoes, thumps and grunts of exertion, and heavy makeup streaming down sweating faces. From my seat in Daly City, ballets looked effortless and ethereal. The reality was quite different. I've always wanted to draw a metaphor from that, something on the order of the Puritan Work Ethic viewed through the wrong end of a telescope. Or, on a more pedestrian level, other people's work may look easy to someone, who's never had to do it.

Jan Schachern's female intuition may have sounded a warning about Mark's rapid elevation within WSB&G and Ed's enthrallment with Mark's potential. The bar business is hard on relationships and family life. She worked at WSB&G long enough to take Ed's measure. She and Mark eventually had four children. Did she fear Mark would become an Ed clone, kibitzing and drinking all day and all night while she tended home, hearth, and cradle? If she had concerns, she was up against a young man, who was bedazzled at the unexpected windfall of becoming a PARTNER in the hottest saloon in the greatest city in the best of times. What could go wrong?

12

Down By the San Francisco Bay

My favorite cover of "San Francisco Bay Blues," which was written by Oakland-based singer/songwriter, Jesse Fuller, was the gravelly-voiced version Richie Havens performed at Woodstock. He soulfully sang,

I got the blues for my baby down by the San Francisco Bay...

Bouts of the blues were rare for me. I had two monogamous affairs, with a few flings in between, so lovelorn blues weren't a big problem. But, emotional ups and downs are part of life. When that happened, the answer was to get out and get moving. The splendor and variety of the City could lift any gloom. The Marina Green was an easy walk from my flat on Octavia. The sight of joggers, kite-fliers, picnickers on the grass, with the Golden Gate Bridge and the Marin Headlands as backdrops were guaranteed blues busters.

The Palace of Fine Arts, with its azure reflecting lagoon, a remnant of the 1915 Panama-Pacific Exhibition, was in walking distance at the other end of the Marina District. A stroll along the Cow Hollow portion of Union Street, peering in the windows of shops and booze dispensaries, was a good diversion.

I had the rare and fortunate blessing for city dwellers of a garage where I kept my MG convertible, so spur-of-the-moment road trips were easily indulged. Put the top down and drive out to the Cliff House, up and down the coast, or off to wine country or Lake Tahoe. Cruise through the green space of the Presidio and hop on 101 to cross Golden Gate Bridge for a change of scene in Sausalito or Tiburon. Or head to Coit Tower atop Telegraph Hill for a panoramic view of the entire Bay area.

Coit Tower was considered a tourist stop, often crowded, and therefore avoided by locals. But, for those well-acquainted with the City, Coit Tower gave a pre-drone, aerial perspective of familiar sights and it was fun to pick out favorite spots. The tower and its property were part of a bequest to the city from Lillie Hitchcock Coit, who was a colorful character in 19th century San Francisco.

Lillie had inherited wealth that allowed her to flamboyantly flaunt the conventions of her time. She wore trousers, smoked cigars, and gambled in men-only establishments. She was enamored with the firefighters of Knickerbocker Engine Co. No. 5. The allure is understandable. The teams of horses that pulled early firefighting equipment were so well-trained they would automatically position themselves under the harnesses, which were suspended from the ceiling and dropped on their backs. The volunteer firemen in dark uniforms were equally prompt. Off the units would go at a gallop, steam belching from the pumper units, firemen clinging to the careening hose and ladder wagons, to fight conflagrations in a city made of wood.

So, great was Lillie's fascination with the Knickerbocker crew, she often rode on the equipment, and supposedly dashed out of her own wedding when she heard the fire bell. In an article for *San*

Francisco Magazine, I referenced the wedding myth and called it Lillie Hitchcock Coitus Interruptus. Virginia "Ginny" Butterfield was the editor of the city magazine and tolerant of my excesses. She said, "That's hilarious, but it will never see the light of day in this magazine."

The ultimate touristy spot was Fisherman's Wharf, which too-cool-for-school locals gave a pass. But I liked making an occasional visit for the sensory pleasures: Croaking sea lions atop barnacle encrusted floating docks with long-green stands of algae wafting in the current. The water-y slap of boats bobbing at their moorings. The clank of rigging on masts. The taste of Dungeness crab with a dollop of Louie sauce in a take away cup purchased from a sidewalk vendor at Alioto's #8. The sight of Alcatraz rising fortress-like from the Bay. The fun of seeing tourists discovering the peripheries of the magic city. And, the smell of bacon.

The fragrance of the breakfast mainstay wafted from the Eagle Cafe, which had been a waterside eatery for fishermen and other blue-collar workers since 1928. The development of Pier 39 threatened its continued existence, but the developers wisely found a place for the Eagle on the second floor of the new addition to Fisherman's Wharf. At that time, the Eagle retained its shabby authenticity and cheap, unpretentious fare. My favorite was the kind of cheese omelet that is rarely seen anymore.

A ladle of yellow goo scooped from a vat of scrambled eggs was poured on a flat grill that is shared with sizzling bacon, sausages, and hash browns. Processed cheese squares are strategically plopped on the yellow circlet. Such omelets bear no resemblance to the carefully-nurtured puffy, pan-made *omellets,* stuffed with tasty ingredients or the fluffy eggs in their cousin the Quiche. The grill-made omelet will be flat and folded like yellow cardboard—and just as tasty. Pass the ketchup, please, and a refill on the brown liquid called coffee. Time capsule Americana.

Pier 39, which opened in 1978, was another no-go zone for many locals. The combination of arcades, amusement park, and knick-knack dispensing shops was thought to be tacky. But, it offered two of my favorite absurdities: a Whack-a-Mole Machine and Bumper Cars. Hal shared my enthusiasm for Whack-a-Mole, but was a little disturbed at how completely I lost it on a Bumper Car Ride. Careening, chasing, bumping, evading, ramming, dodging, in the little cars, while howling with laughter, is so cathartic. Those activities should be folded into Marriage Counseling and Anger Management. No way stress, hostility, or hard feelings can survive that crazy fun.

Another option for beating the blues by getting out and about, was the Muni bus, which stopped near my apartment building. The route, which passed through Chinatown, was convenient for meeting friends for *dim sum*. The labor-intensive steamed dumplings and mini munches had just become available. Or I might hop off the bus to buy one of the roast ducks displayed in store windows. After selecting one of the mahogany-colored ducks, the butcher would section it with expert whacks of a meat cleaver, and package it, ready to enjoy at home.

Often, the sidewalks were crowded with live creatures for Chinese women to prepare at home. Once, I saw an abalone trying to ooze its way over the top of a cooler. The will to escape was there, but not the speed.

Another time, an elderly Chinese woman boarded the Muni bus with a chicken under her arm. The bus driver made it clear that she couldn't bring a live animal on the bus. She glared at him, grabbed the chicken by the head, and with a quick snap of her wrist, broke its neck. She tucked the limp bird back under her elbow and said, "Okay, now?"

The Muni bus route would proceed to Union Square, the premiere shopping area of the City interspersed with luxury hotels, where a transfer could easily be made to one of the famous San Francisco cable cars for a rattling, bell-clanging return down the hills. Locals avoided the cable cars, which were so popular with tourists filling the seats or clinging to the outside, it was nearly impossible to find a spot.

Much of the year, the cable car turnarounds, like the one at Market and Powell, were thronged with tourists, who seemed oblivious to the antiquated technology of the conveyance they were so anxious to board. There are only three remaining cable car lines from the original system that was built in 1873. Indeed, the San Francisco cable car system is the only one left in the world.

The mechanism is still the same; a *grip* under the car grips or clamps onto a continuous underground cable driven by an engine at a central powerhouse. When descending a steep hill like Powell Street, the grip is all that stands between a pleasant ride and an out-of-control juggernaut into the Bay. Relax and enjoy the view, folks!

Even with all those options for getting out and enjoying the city, I thought I'd like to have a bicycle—a notion that was ill-fated from the start. I bought a ten-speed, but not the kind used by serious cyclists with dropped handlebars and no aerodynamic hindrances. Mine was a granny version that had straight handlebars and a bracket on the back wheel with a hinged clamp for carrying small items.

When an acquaintance learned I'd bought a bike, he suggested we ride together. We had some lovely outings to the Embarcadero, and around the Financial District on Sundays when the streets were nearly deserted, and over Golden Gate Bridge. When I began dating a mutual friend, my biker buddy became angry, said I'd been leading him on, and called a halt to our excursions. Such was the tangled state of affairs between men and women in the 1980s that bike riding was considered foreplay.

However, I kept riding my bike. With a chain and padlock, it was handy for running errands. Or so I thought. I put several rented video tapes and a bank deposit containing $500 cash in a bag under the clamp and set off for a ride around the neighborhood to include the video rental store and the Wells Fargo Bank on Chestnut Street. When I arrived at the bank, the clamp was empty. I backtracked but couldn't find the tapes or the cash. Not only was I out hard-earned money, but I'd have to pay for the tapes.

Amazingly, I got phone call a few days later from the employees at a gas station who found the lost items, tracked me down through the video store, and returned everything. And they refused a reward.

Since the clamp had betrayed me, I decided to carry shopping items in a canvas tote over the handle bars, the kind with straps that KQED gave out during the pledge drive. I had just turned off Union Street onto Octavia, which was slightly downhill. The edge of the canvas bag slipped into the spokes and stopped the bike more effectively than the brakes ever did. I was pitched over the handlebars and plopped onto the asphalt. A kindly observer rushed over to check on me.

When it was determined I was just scraped and humiliated, he began urging me to "Get back on! Just get right back on!" the advice usually given to horseback riders who've been bucked off. I appreciated his concern but told him "It's a Schwinn. Not Secretariat."

I'd had it with the bike, which seemed possessed by bad juju. I announced at work I was selling it—cheap—but any buyer should know the damn thing was demonic. Waiter Steve Cieply was happy to buy it, but scoffed at my wild imagination. Steve rode the bike home, parked it for five minutes outside his apartment, where it was promptly stolen.

Unlike Sam Dietsch, who got the jitters if he stepped outside North Beach, I occasionally left the City for brief excursions. In February, 1986, I flew to Anchorage, Alaska—yes, February—for an event called the Fur Rendezvous, which celebrates trappers gathering to sell their pelts. The "Rondy" also featured sled dog races. At an unseasonably mild 12 degrees, there wasn't enough snow to run the races, but snow was trucked onto a main street for dog sled demonstrations. For the locals, 12 degrees was T-shirt weather. Bundled in my polar expedition clothing purchased at an Army-Navy surplus store in San Francisco, I was clearly "Lower 48."

Anchorage had adopted the moose as a Chamber of Commerce totem. Moose pins, moose T-shirts, memorabilia, and tourist trinkets of all kinds were everywhere. Despite the warm-fuzziness of the moose knick-knacks, a local warned me that moose are extremely dangerous and given a wide berth by Alaskans. Nevertheless, I wanted to see one of the great creatures in the wild and rented a car to sightsee outside the city limits. After hours of moose-less travel, I returned to Anchorage and drove into a traffic jam created by a mother moose with her calf munching from a dumpster behind a pizza joint.

I rolled down the car window and asked a person parked next to me "What happens now?" He replied "Absolutely nothing, unless you want your car torn apart." When around moose, use caution. Yeah, I had that one down.

Another time, I flew to Santa Fe, New Mexico, for a few days of land of enchantment scenery, art gallery viewing, local color, drinking and dining. Marcy said The Pink Adobe, a Mexican restaurant situated in a centuries' old adobe house, was a must for dinner. I have a foggy memory of the charming Pink Adobe. Something about beamed ceilings, little blaze crackling in a kiva fireplace, excellent steak and a half bottle of red wine. Why so foggy?

Prior to my dinner reservation, I went to the bar at La Fonda Hotel for a margarita. Two fish bowl sized margaritas appeared—it was happy hour. One simply does not leave a margarita (or two) unfinished. That bravado plus Santa Fe's altitude (7,199 feet above sea level) knocked me for a loop and obscured my dining experience at The Pink Adobe. Famed San Francisco bar keep, Morty Miller, used to say "'Don't ruin a 10 dollar heat with a 20 dollar dinner." Prices adjusted for inflation, still good advice.

I took a pass on my best opportunity for visiting Australia. My brother, Jeff Berkley, who's traveled the world in a field called deep ocean engineering, worked for two years on a tourist submarine project in Perth, Western Australia. The length of the flight with my chronic back problems was just too daunting. However, everyone went a bit Aussie crazy when the film *The Man from Snowy River* came out in 1982. The stockmen chasing the brumbies wore oilskin dusters, which had not previously been seen.

I asked Jeff to purchase one and ship it to me. When I went walkabout on the streets of San Francisco wearing the duster, people tried to buy it off my back. There were countless name-your-price offers.

When the Perth project concluded, Jeff and his wife Carol Ann took a chartered sailing vacation in the Maldives, then stopped in San Francisco for a sibling reunion. One evening, they were craving Thai food, so we went to a local Thai restaurant. I was unfamiliar with the cuisine, so Jeff ordered several entrees to share and a couple items from an extensive curry menu. I loved the flavors.

Therefore, when an out-of-town friend visited a couple weeks later, I suggested dinner at the same Thai restaurant. I reordered the main dishes my brother had chosen, but consulting the curry menu, I was at a loss, and didn't understand the selections from one to 40 indicated escalating hotness, specifically tongue-numbing, esophagus-scorching fire, not for the uninitiated—or some ethnicities. Winging it, I ordered 25 and 38. The Thai waiter shook his head emphatically and said "No 38 for round eye."

Whether getting out and about to beat the blues or traveling for fun and diversions, a great meal or unusual restaurant can mark the occasions. Top of my list is Louie's Backyard in Key West. My family made the 120-mile trek from mainland Florida to Key West back in the days when the bridges were made of wood and it seemed perilous to lose sight of dry land. Sharks and sea life were clearly visible swimming underneath the timbered bridges.

By 1975, the bridges were all concrete and Key West seemed like a good inaugural drive for my newly purchased MG. I did the usual tourist sights and arrived at Louie's Backyard at dusk where I'd requested a table on the patio. With the Atlantic Ocean on the left and the Gulf of Mexico on the right, I watched the sun sink below the horizon while savoring frog legs and a half bottle of Pouilly Fuisse. Louie's is still there, ditto the ocean, the gulf, and the unforgettable sunsets.

Another Florida restaurant, sadly out of business, was memorable, The Studio in Coral Gables. A cavernous, low-ceilinged space with Continental fare, The Studio had a distinctly quirky staff and apparently imaginative management. Waiters and waitresses were allowed to wear whatever costumes they chose: Pirate. Cowboy. Belly dancer. Nurse. Vampire. A friend had introduced me to The Studio. Subsequently I took Hal there. The service was efficient, lively, and just the right amount of engaging. Hal was instantly charmed and we both felt we'd entered a place that had a bit of WSB&G magic.

In the early days, Washington Square Bar & Grill was building a reputation as a place worth traveling to, but not for the food. The food critics were unkind, relentlessly it seemed, as though an eatery that was succeeding without their approval was fair game for shaming.

Restaurant reviews and food critics are part of publications in big city life. They serve a purpose as consumer guidelines, but some of them could make or break a new business at the most vulnerable time—just getting started.

I recall a place on Chestnut Street, which was being renovated. I'd peek in the windows to watch the progress. Like many startups, it probably represented an individual's dream, which investors were willing to fund, not the sort of corporatization that's now common. Shortly after opening, one of the City's foodies reviewed the place and ridiculed a silly incident.

Apparently, a dish was served with a *jardinere* of baby vegetables. When the critic attempted to put a fork into a baby beet, the al dente veggie leaped off the plate and rolled along the floor. The critic ridiculed the purple escapee excessively, to the point it defined the restaurant. The new venture had a rough start and I don't recall if they ever recovered.

The foodies got a hilarious comeuppance when they wildly lauded a restaurant in Boonville that supposedly grew all its own vegetables. "Locally sourced" was an important component of Californian Cuisine, and what could be more locally sourced than a garden plot right outside the kitchen door? Eventually, someone calculated the square footage of the garden couldn't possibly have supplied the restaurant's needs.

Boonville, in the Anderson Valley of Mendocino County, is notable as an enclave of people who speak Boontling, a jargon created in the 1890s by farmworkers. Very few people remain who speak Boontling, but I imagine this conversation:

"Hey, Ma, here comes a car full of food critics. Put on your bonnet and apron, go stand by the road, and pull some carrots."

Disparaging the fare at WSB&G occupied the foodies for many years. The food was never bad. When the saloon was opened on Labor Day 1973, Aldo Persich, a well-respected North Beach chef, was in charge of the kitchen. The new owners had not planned to compete with other established Italian restaurants in North Beach, but the menu of grilled hamburgers and French fries they envisioned gave way to Aldo's skill set. Four years later, when I was hired, the dishes that came from the kitchen were reliably satisfying. Yet, grumblings about the cuisine continued. Were the food critics miffed that their discourses on Balsamic vinegar and rolling beets failed to deter the common folk from patronizing WSB&G?

Even the non-professional foodies had to take their shots. A 1986 article in *California Magazine* by mega-writer, Orville Schell, continues to amuse. With a party of eight other writers, Mr. Schell and crew sought to ascertain if WSB&G was, as advertised, a writers' hangout. The research was conducted during the melee that was a typical WSB&G power lunch where the crowds, noise, and manic pace, weren't conducive to elegant flourishes. Large parties always add extra stress on a kitchen.

After concluding there were no writers present—irony duly noted—the writers became food critics. Longtime host of the radio show *West Coast Live,* Sedge Thomson, described the food as "neutral" and the service as "slap down." Reportedly, the service was also slap down when the last plane left Saigon.

Author John Krich described his veal scallopini piccata with capers as "[I]nstitutional…the boiler plate stuff that has been sating unsuspecting North Beach tourists for decades—what we were satisfied to accept as Italian before the discovery of virgin olive oil, sun-dried tomatoes and goat cheese calzone."

Piccata, the lemony-buttery, white wine and capers, sauce is a classic of Italian cookery, one might say "institutional" so the criticism was perplexing. Personally, I'd eat a tennis shoe sautéed piccata style. And, the classics wax and wane to be rediscovered by the next generation of chefs. But, the nub of the Schell & Co. article had been arrived at: Not nouvelle enough.

The California Cuisine that emanated from Chez Panisse, Alice Waters' Berkeley restaurant, was being incorporated at most eateries and was expected by would-be foodies. Sweep those classics off the table! The insistence that WSB&G should jump on the bandwagon of California Cuisine was called "panise envy" by the staff. And, was typical of the weird San Francisco mentality that to demonstrate one's individuality, it was necessary to join the latest trends as quickly as possible.

By 1986, when Orville Schell's writers-turned-foodies piece was published, the WSB&G kitchen, under the direction of Mary Etta Moose, had been expanding its vocabulary for years. And good reviews had become the norm. Innovation and "institutional" coexisted.

Mary Etta had made a study of cookery and food that went back to the early years of her romance with Ed when she has an absolute beginner. The Mooses were fond of telling a story from their days in St. Louis. When Woody Allen was a young comic appearing at the Crystal Palace, Ed and Mary Etta invited him for a home-cooked meal, Mary Etta's chili. The taste was so shocking, Woody froze. When he was able to recover, he asked, "Can you get polio from chili?"

Mary Etta constantly added, subtracted, and adjusted, the menu to reflect what she knew about WSB&G clientele, keeping the selections affordable, and balancing comfortable favorites with dishes for more sophisticated palates. In 1981, Mary Etta's expertise was sufficiently respected that she collaborated with author and wine expert, Brian St. Pierre, to write a book entitled *The Flavor of North Beach*, which sketched in the history of North Beach, visited a number of favorite restaurants, and offered chef's recipes tailored for home cooks. A revised version of the popular book is still available.

Time spent with Brian, who was always cheerful and charming, both of them discussing topics they loved, must have been affirming for Mary Etta. The amount of time spent with Ed, or Edward as she always called him, seemed to be scant. He spent long hours during lunch and dinner service at WSB&G seven days a week. When Mary Etta was at WSB&G, she was upstairs in the cramped office, working on tasks, menus, ordering from purveyors, and taking her meals up there.

The staff would have been happy to serve her lunch and even a luncheon party of her friends. I don't recall that ever happening. It wasn't appropriate to try to be chummy with the Boss's Wife. While Mary Etta was always cordial to staff in a distant way, none of us felt well-acquainted with her.

However, females on the staff worried that Mary Etta led a lonely life—part consort, part personal assistant, and part keeper of the flame. At a time when young women were embracing feminist principles of equal opportunity, equal pay for equal work, and refuting sexual harassment and second-class treatment in the workplace, Mary Etta seemed subservient to Edward's alpha male agenda.

In a 1985 *Examiner* article, writer Jim Wood, interviewed Ed and Mary Etta on the topic of relationship between spouses, who work together. Wood called them "a magic team." For female staffers, reading between the lines, the article validated concerns about Mary Etta's constrained life. Although reading between the number of lines allotted to Mary Etta made for a short study.

For two pages in the Style section Ed talked about himself, name dropped about famous friends, and made the inevitable reference to his softball team. Mary Etta seemed afflicted with Stockholm Syndrome in print, but was permitted space to comment about working together "It's hard enough to balance your married life without trying to balance a business partnership simultaneously."

To which Edward replied, "I think it's a flatout mistake. I don't think anybody should work together." With that chivalry fail behind him, Ed revealed a bit about their time together outside of work:

> *Mary Etta: We travel, we love the theater. We're in New York and London as often as we can for the theater.*
> *Jim Wood: How often is that?*
> *Edward: I go four to six times a year. Mary Etta goes…*
> *Mary Etta: About once.*

At one of the annual staff Christmas parties, which hats off to our bosses were wonderful, I decided on a tribute to Mary Etta. Her birthday fell near Christmas and most children similarly born feel short-changed about celebrations of their natal day. So, I illustrated a giant birthday card to be the centerpiece of the party that showed two cartoon moose driving an old, red jalopy through a snowy landscape. One moose wore a tweed cap between its antlers and the Mary Etta Moose had ringlets of black hair under a ski cap. In the rumble seat was a cartoon Sam. The red car was at an intersection marked with an old-fashioned wooden sign pointing in different directions: Merry Christmas and Happy Birthday.

Mary Etta seemed pleased.

While I thought Mary Etta was underappreciated, I was often irked at how little recognition Sam got. For me, he was the genuine wit and scrappy warmth at the heart of WSB&G. Oh, he was always mentioned in any article about WSB&G. There was always an obligatory mention of "partner Sam Deitsch" but, some writers even failed to spell his name correctly.

Yet, Sam seemed unfazed by Ed taking all the bows. I never saw a moment of envy or discontent from him. Instead, of lionizing the famous drive-by patrons of WSB&G, Sam enjoyed the neighborhood characters, interesting regulars, and working folks, who formed a large block of customers that were comfortable coming in for a couple drinks and a schmooze.

Sometimes, Sam mimicked the role of effusive host with poseurs, who approached him. As they extended a handshake, Sam would gush an extravagant greeting that sounded like "HOW are you?" but was actually "WHO are you?"

Sam had made a success of the Golden Eagle in Gaslight Square in St. Louis. Perhaps, those were laurels he was content to rest upon. That success had brought the WSB&G trio together and initiated everything that would happen in North Beach. That might have enough for Sam. In the truest act of friendship, he may have been willing to allow his friend Ed, whose resume theretofore was absent much in the way of laurels, to throw himself into creating something wildly successful with Ed's imprimatur.

Examiner columnist, Rob Morse, was usually cranky on the subject of WSB&G and particularly Ed Moose. In a 1986 column, he wrote "Ed Moose of the you-know-what-bag left on an African safari last week. He told his staff that if he were to be kidnapped by terrorists that no one should negotiate or pay any ransom. What makes him think anyone would want to?"

Uh, I would want to. And just about everyone else that wanted an extraordinary phenomenon to continue.

Jesse Fuller's San Francisco Bay Blues, made grindingly plaintive by Richie Havens' voice, is a song about lost love, but holds out hope:

> *I got the blues for my baby down by the San Francisco Bay.*
> *An ocean liner took her so far away*
> *If she ever comes back to stay, gonna be another*
> *   brand-new day*
> *When I go walkin' with my baby*
> *Down by the San Francisco Bay.*

After years of wanderlust, I thought the City would be my permanent home. I was there to stay. I thought I'd always be walkin' down by the San Francisco Bay. Side trips provided release valves for travel desires, but leaving the City was unthinkable. Until it wasn't.

13

The Times Were A-Changing

Hal Thunes and I were taking a short break during a busy evening when a big bosomed woman entered wearing a thin blouse. The "boobs" were unrestrained and rolled around under the blouse like battling watermelons. Hal prided himself on having seen it all, but he nudged me:

> *Hal: Do you think she would fail the pencil test?*
> *Me: What's that?*
> *Hal: The feminists say if a woman puts a pencil under her*
>   *breast and it stays there, she is too big to go without a bra.*
> *Me: Really? I'd say she would fail the typewriter test.*

Feminist "Waves" were washing over society. Was San Francisco in the 1980s still part of the first wave? Was it second wave? Was it a tide pool? The bar business was not an area where women's issues and feminist intellectuals were studied. Thus, the optics could be, and continue to be, confusing. The no-bra look of the women's libber, who failed the typewriter test, what was that about? How did rallies of buck nekkid women address women's equality demands? Have pink vagina hats advanced the political cause?

The women of WSB&G, unassisted by optics or feminist treatises, were self-actualizing feminists. The famous saloon was our boot camp. We didn't think of ourselves as fighting the good sisterhood fight, we were just trying to stand our ground. Every day we dealt with unequal treatment, sexual advances from men (and women) and issues about seniority and performance based on merit. We managed with spirit and humor, probably schooled a few boorish dudes—and even edified some of the higher ups.

Sam could be relied on to appreciate the women staffers. But taking grievances to him about his partner's seeming bias against women, would have put him in an untenable position. It wasn't appropriate to ask Sam to function as HR—or to appeal to Mary Etta. Mark was Ed's wingman, so that was a No. As Ed moved from mildly chauvinistic in the early days to more overtly misogynistic in the late 1980s, female staffers were becoming a minority by the addition of more and more male employees on the floor and behind the bar.

The women servers added substantially to WSB&G's bottom line and did so without the shenanigans of the bartenders, who were Ed's band of brothers. At 10 o'clock, it was their custom to stop what they were doing and have shots of Green Chartreuse, a 110-proof jolt, which was not their first drink of their shift. Gambling, their wins, losses, and outstanding wagers, occupied much of their conversation. Sofi recalled an unusual evening when no games or gambling activity of any kind was available. A rare bettors' desert! So, the bartenders organized a pool to bet on how many dinners would be served that night.

We loved our bartenders and didn't object to their choices of entertainment. They filled our drink orders promptly and were part of Family Table fun. But, they considered bartending to be a step above food service. Thus, when union problems began, they sided with Ed, leaving us burgeoning feminists to take the heat. If they thought they were exempt from Ed's dark side, they should have consulted Hal and Cyril.

From my childhood, I could recognize tyranny, even the petty kind Ed repeatedly tried to impose. I was familiar with the injustice of being a model child, trying to follow the rules, and to do my job well, yet still being found insufficient. I deflected Ed's mean-spirited stunts for years, while remaining deferential. When I was hired, Ed had been a restauranteur four years. I'd been in the business for 17 years. So, Ed wasn't my first eccentric boss.

Out of respect, I always pointed out notable people to him and kept Ed informed on matters he cared about. I was dutiful but guarded. He was a Dodge Ball Boss, but still the boss. Despite my attempted propriety, Ed decided to appropriate a chunk of my income and give it to Mark Schachern.

The partnership arrangement Mark had entered, proved financially inadequate for the support of his family. Ed's solution was that Mark would return to being a waiter several nights a week. Not a waiter that donned a tuxedo, clocked in at 6 pm and worked until 11 pm, as we all did. But a waiter, who would take premium tables at 8 pm in the best station, work for two hours (long enough to secure the right to tips from those tables) then leave the tables for other waiters to finish. Then, Mark would change back into his partner clothes and resume schmoozing at the bar. And the food server, who was chosen to have the cream skimmed off the top, was me.

Perhaps, there was a perception that I made more money than others. That distinction probably went to Bobby Ryder by virtue of the many hours and shifts he covered, but Ed certainly wouldn't suggest his young partner be subjected to Bobby's crazy schedule. Instead, the primo station at the front of the dining room with the coveted window tables that I had earned through seniority, was the target. Ed felt my income was fair game for the financial shortfall in his misbegotten partnership with Mark.

Besides being unjust, the plan was logistically unworkable, and might have disrupted the flow of the entire dining room. Clearly, it was a bully move by a boss, who'd never waited on tables. The staff also thought it was a humiliating, bully move against Mark. Whatever Mark's expectations were of becoming a partner in WSB&G, it probably didn't include stepping backwards into the ranks of food servers, waiting in line for cocktails at the service bar, and sweating the heat of the kitchen to collect his food orders. He was supposed to be the boss of all those people, not one of them.

Undoubtedly, Mark knew he was a pawn. But, what could he do? He'd bet his future on the fortunes of WSB&G. In a city where great restaurants came and went, he must have thought WSB&G would go on forever. And, he'd tied himself to Ed Moose, who had demonstrated that his loyalty fluctuated as much as his alcohol-fueled blood sugar.

Furthermore, Mark was allegedly in hock to Sam for $50,000. According to a later report, Mark <u>bought</u> his 10% partnership with a loan from Sam. The claim, from a highly credible source, is perplexing. Sam didn't seem particularly close to Mark. If the business needed a cash infusion, why wouldn't Sam do it directly? Was Sam pressured to dig into his pocket by Ed to add this supposedly essential new partner?

Whatever the behind-the-scenes partnership arrangements were, I was fed up with Ed's vindictive Dodge Ball. Like the corrosive

174

episode where my mother stripped the clothes off my back, Ed was asserting that I was nothing but what he'd given me, and he could take back those behests at will. In my view, Ed was doing the same thing to Mark, and his *hubris* was erasing Sam.

As a child I'd had no recourse. But, I did then. Time to throw down the union card. Washington Square Bar & Grill was a union shop (Local 2, Hotel and Restaurant Workers). For years, I'd watched Ed squeeze every drop of back-slapping, political favoritism, Democrat-networking, and phony man-of-the-people, benefit from the union connection—until he wanted to flout the most basic rules of worker protection. He was a long way from his do-gooder days.

I met with Ed in the upstairs office, just the two of us. I was quaking inside. But I was done with the feeling instilled by my mother that I had no intrinsic value. I told Ed I was going to file a complaint with Local 2 about his move to install Mark in my station. I stated it plainly and resisted the female impulse to explain or justify. As Hal told me many years earlier, "Sometimes the only correct answer is No." Ed was red-faced and fuming on the outside, and probably volcanic on the inside, but rescinded his punitive action.

While undercurrents were stirring beneath the surface, the public saw WSB&G proceed as the crazy-wonderful Soap Opera and never-a-dull-moment Fun House everyone loved. The Cal Band, one hundred strong (Go Bears!) still marched through the saloon a few days prior to the big Cal-Stanford game, rattling the old building with fight songs, compliments of Jack Brown, a wealthy furniture company executive and Cal Band superfan.

From boisterous band concerts to quiet but joyous affairs, anything was possible at the beloved venue, like the wedding of

Mike Greensill and Wesla Whitfield in 1986. Mike was a regular pianist at WSB&G, but that was just a fragment of his talents and history. When he heard Wesla singing at a local cabaret, he made her acquaintance, and eventually became her arranger and accompanist.

Wesla was an extraordinary singer—and survivor. At the age of 29, she was paralyzed from the waist down by a random gunshot, but that didn't stop her career from ascending to prestigious jazz clubs in New York, to Carnegie Hall, and even the White House, a journey she made with Mike. When the two were joined in matrimony at WSB&G, Mike noted how convenient it was to have a good stiff drink before saying "I do."

Dick Fregulia recalls a woman, who requested he play the lovely Michele LeGrand song "What Are You Doing the Rest of Your Life?" He complied with a sensitive rendition. Shortly after, the woman returned, crying happy tears to tell Dick her boyfriend had just proposed.

The wedding theme was in keeping with another memorable event. An engaged couple was having dinner when a Prohibition Era sedan pulled up at the front door. The running boards were festooned with tough guys dressed in pin striped suits and Fedoras, carrying plastic Tommy guns. They burst through the door and captured the startled bridegroom—for his bachelor party.

Actual criminals also preferred WSB&G. Two people showed up for a late lunch. They requested a window table and said they would wait until one became available. Shortly after they were seated, the police arrived and arrested them. The duo had robbed a local market and were using the loot to buy lunch.

On any given Sunday, a pop-up concert featuring notable jazz musicians could enrich the brunch and Bloody Mary experience. The gigs were more charming for, what seemed like, their impromptu nature. Pianists Lou Levy, Dave Frishberg, Bob

Dorough, and Eubie Blake, were they just passing through the City? Did drummer, Shelly Manne, and saxophone greats, Stan Getz and Al Cohn, hear through the grape vine there would be a musical happening at WSB&G?

The events must have involved pre-planning. Regulars were apprised, jazz fans got the memos, musicians gathered, but the seemingly spontaneous musical delights enhanced WSB&G's reputation as a place of infinite variety.

While I was treated to jazz every evening at work, I was a rock and roller at heart. The music of the 1980s included my favorites: Eagles, Journey, Doobie Brothers, Dire Straits, and homegrown hotties, Huey Lewis and the News, Carlos Santana, and Boz Scaggs. Neil was wildly enthused about a new guy he called The Boss, Bruce Springsteen. Tunes were available at Tower Records at Bay and Columbus.

In 1984, Sofi quit, after eight years as the female dynamo of WSB&G. Her energy, sharply-expressed insights, and distinctive laugh, were sorely missed. She cited Ed's lack of respect for the women staffers as one reason for leaving. But her affection for Sam was undiminished. When she married several years later, she asked Sam to give her away—at ceremonies in Alameda. Ed expressed skepticism that Sam would leave North Beach, especially for a destination like Alameda.

He was wrong. Sam made the trip two days in a row, for the rehearsal and the wedding. His co-pilot, Patsy Glynn, the feisty trial lawyer, who drew Ed's ire for speaking up at a softball game, had become his steady girlfriend. She was funny and bright and the two of them connected over shared interests and mutual love of the saloon life. With Patsy's help, Sam's horizon was enlarged to include Alameda. In preparation for the epic trek, Patsy went to a liquor store and loaded up on airline-size bottles of booze. Fortified with Dutch Courage and pockets full of hooch, Sam was there for Sofi. The bride wore white. Sam wore—the usual.

Arlene was one of those people, who don't immediately put all their cards on the table. Prior to joining the staff at WSB&G, she'd been a truck driver (her father was a teamster) but she also attended art school in Detroit and California. Her creative evolution was ongoing. When she married bartender and smart guy, Michael Boyle, the pair bought a Victorian in the Western Addition.

Her flair for interior decorating was unique. A large painting by our co-worker, Debbie Lawder Sullivan, dominated the living room. In the bathroom was a photo collage of Country Western singers, including Waylon and Willie and the Boys. Merle Haggard's photo had the place of honor by the toilet paper holder. Eventually, Arlene founded a successful florist business that specialized in weddings, and bore a personally significant name: Violetta Flowers.

While Arlene gave off a city-dweller vibe, she also boarded a horse at a Hidden Valley Ranch on Cull Canyon Road in the East Bay. Arlene invited Marcy and me for country get togethers we called the One-Horse Equestrian Club. When Arlene became pregnant, she asked if I wanted to lease her horse, which meant I would pay the board, veterinary, and horse shoeing expenses. I jumped at the chance to realize a childhood dream.

Hidden Valley Ranch abutted 50,000 acres of public land, some of the best riding territory imaginable. The rolling hills, covered with dun colored grass, had been compared by a poet to "the backs of sleeping lions." Valley oaks with sweeping branches provided shade and beauty. Dirt roads that criss-crossed the vast expanse, made it possible to ride a horse from Skyline Drive in the Oakland Hills all the way to Danville where a bar provided a hitching post for thirsty equestrians. I began to feel the old itch for something different.

The Lapin Sauvages, Ed's softball team, was still travelling to more and more exotic destinations and still getting lots of media coverage. Herb Caen's enthusiasm as a columnist and a player, meant he was always good for ink. Ron Fimrite's variations on a theme seemed inexhaustible. (How many times can one write that Ed's preferred ball players had to be over 40 years of age or have a bad liver?) After so many years, the headlines for yet another game should have read "Select Few Take Trips That You Never Will."

But, if anyone thought the softball shtick was getting shopworn, it would have been heresy to say so. How much interest could the general readership sustain for Ed Moose and his band of boozy ballers? The editors, who repeatedly okayed yet another softball story for a diminishing audience, must have thought the French peasants were interested in what Marie Antoinette was having for lunch.

However, Les Lapins Sauvages continued as a reliable device in Ed's PR bag of tricks. When Ed needed attention (a near constant condition) he would announce a new match that required travel arrangements and coverage. When he again needed attention, Ed would announce the team was retiring. In 1983, *California Living* ran an article, with a cover illustration by Dugald Stermer of a fielder's glove and a tattered softball, which read "The Washbag Hangs It Up."

In 1984, the team played the Media All Stars during the Democrat Convention and ink ran in the streets. In 1986, *Image Magazine* published a five-page piece with 14 photos on the Wild Rabbits. Even as the union dispute was unfolding, Ed planned a softball trip to Moscow. Les Lapins Sauvages had more deaths and resurrections than Lazarus on teeter totter.

Alone among the City's columnists, who rested comfortably in the palm of Ed's hand, the *Examiner's* Rob Morse seems to have sniffed out Ed's phony bonhomie. About the endless flogging of the softball team, he wrote, "Since this team was concocted by barroom draft in 1979, it has received more coverage—starting with *Sports Illustrated*—than the San Francisco Giants. In past years, this may have been fitting, but no more."

But, in 1987, Ed's team got a comeuppance from an unlikely quarter—his own employees. The scheme was hatched by Neil Riofski. His talent for presenting outstanding celebrations like his Bum Touts Party for failed race horse bettors and his Birthday Bash spiced with his jokes and stories, was famous among his admirers and friends. He proposed a softball game between WSB&G staffers and the boss's vaunted Lapin Sauvages.

In typical Neil fashion, no detail was overlooked. He chose the team name, Base Carnards, delightful for its double meaning. If the Lapin Sauvages were the Wild Rabbits, we would be the "Bad Ducks," feathered foes but also a hoax or false report. Neil gave me the job of designing T-shirts. For our mascot, I created an angry, cigar-smoking duck with one webbed foot on a base and its wings defiantly akimbo. The challenge was accepted and scheduled for a baseball diamond off Stanyan Street in Golden Gate Park. (No home field advantage for the Wild Rabbits!)

Neil was the coach and had his strategy pre-planned. I showed up at the game with Mike Clark, a guy I met horseback riding in the East Bay hills. He was a Vietnam Vet and a superb horseman. He claimed to have tried out for the Oakland A's in the 1970s and made the team. But, I hadn't dated him long enough to know if that was a tall tale.

I asked Neil if Mike could play. Neil was skeptical about a roster change for a newcomer, but said he would put Mike in as catcher for a few innings. My new beau said "Babe, catcher is for dummies."

I urged him to accept the position graciously and do the best he could. Mike's play and athleticism helped the Bad Ducks crush the Wild Rabbits. He leaped upwards and crashed into the backstop to snag a foul ball that no amateur would even have attempted. He had numerous RBIs from hitting a homerun and a double. And, from home base, he made outs and double plays.

Ed was apoplectic, yelling "Ringer! Ringer!" calling for rules' checks, and claiming his best players weren't present. Neil was jubilant at the rout, but given Ed's unsportsmanlike conduct, declined a rematch. Nor did any of us disagree. We saw the tantrums, rants, pouting, and childish petulance, his softball team were familiar with. We would soon see that behavior again as a union dispute approached.

"L'etat c'est moi."...Louis XIV
"WSB&G is Ed Moose."...The Media

Eventually, Ed chafed at the costs of running a union shop. By 1987, the cost benefit of good public relations via union connections in a Democrat-run city was running headlong into the costs of doing business. Ed decided to focus on his financial obligations to the union as the reason WSB&G wasn't generating the net income he thought it should. The basic arrangement was that waiters, busboys, and bartenders, worked for less than minimum wage, because tips, presumably, made up the difference. The food servers, as is customary, gave a significant amount of their tips to busboys and bartenders. All of us paid monthly dues to Local 2. Ed paid monthly for health benefits for each employee for a union program with Kaiser Permanente. Employer contributions also funded pensions for retired workers.

Rising health costs (when are they not?) and retired worker pensions were both irksome to Ed. The days of being a do-gooder, when he sought to spend taxpayer and charitable funds to uplift the downtrodden, were behind him. His money, aka profits, were a different matter. Uplifting had become heavy lifting. He wanted to go non-union and could see no other way to get costs under control.

Apparently, Ed couldn't see (or be led by a guide dog and a white cane) to cost cutting measures that were his responsibility. Over-spending on non-essentials was obvious. Such as, the practice of printing menus for lunch and dinner every day. The menu was fairly static except for the daily specials, which waiters could have recited or a white board announced. Yet, the menus, printed on heavy card stock and embellished with Larry Green's art work, arrived daily from the printer, sometimes perilously close to the start of business. The reason for this expensive practice? Ed said it was a San Francisco tradition.

Food costs were another factor. From the outset, quality products were a priority. In the restaurant business, it's thought that backing away from quality is a fatal mistake. But, menus can be reconfigured, purchases adjusted, and lemonade made from lemons. While that would have been a big task, was it considered or attempted?

What about rent? The original rent when the Pistola business was acquired, was $300, and that was before the tropical fish store was added. How much did the rent increase? While rent control helped working people stay in their apartments, there was no such rent protection for business owners. As WSB&G's fame grew, the landlord, of course, would want higher and higher compensation for the property.

Once again, the waggish comment, "The only thing worse than failure is success" was in play. WSB&G had succeeded beyond all expectations and the unforeseen costs of success, such as taxes, property and liability insurance, may have blind-sided the owners. With all that, shifting the blame away from management was unseemly, but Deflection Dodge Ball was the order of the day.

The employees resented bearing sole responsibility for runaway costs, especially when advertising and PR consultants remained big ticket items in the budget. Ed was probably as adept as any of the flacks he employed. WSB&G was the most famous saloon in the City, constantly referenced in the local media and written about in national publications. Yet, astonishingly, a giant billboard appeared in downtown San Francisco announcing a business called Washington Square Bar & Grill, which must have been aimed at the one person in the City, who was not yet aware of Ed's place. Not since the billboard in *The Great Gatsby* had there been such inexplicable signage.

How Ed spent company money was his affair by virtue of being the Large Fromage. A Self-Aggrandizement Surcharge for billboards and such, was his choice. By the late 1980s, it's unlikely that anyone else nominally in WSB&G's management, could pump the brakes of Ed's swagger. A fawning media had inflated his sense of brilliance and infallibility. Certainly, his charisma was an important factor in WSB&G's success, but a business also needs a green eyeshade guy with a red pencil. Who, if anyone, filled that unglamorous role? Or could get through to Ed?

Local 2 offered to look at the books and advise based on the accumulated knowledge of running union shops in the City. (Ed must have recoiled from that idea like Dracula confronted with a garlic pizza.) Was a professional management consultant considered? Doubtful. A subjective forensic report might have been unflattering.

No, a fight with the union and his own staff was the path Ed was clearly on. Unless, the staff was willing to accept a health program that Ed believed he could secure at more reasonable rates, and agree to back off seniority and other worker perks, there would be war.

On September 12, 1987, Mike Clark and I were married in Reno, Nevada. The decade I spent at WSB&G came to an end. New adventures, new places, and new people were ahead. I left my friends and wonderful colleagues, with a warning based on my experiences: Ed cannot be trusted.

14
How The Stars Fell

In 1989, Ron Fimrite's book, *The Square,* was published. While he was writing his book, Mike and I were living in Washington State where we moved in late 1987 to buy horse property and to be closer to my brother, who lived in British Columbia. The Pacific Northwest has many charms, but Californians, who are accustomed to fabulous weather almost every day, don't transplant well. We met wonderful people and loved the horse community, but the rain became too much for us. After two years, we washed out and returned to the Bay Area, horses and all.

Our return in late fall, was shortly after the Loma Prieta earthquake had collapsed portions of the Nimitz Expressway and the Oakland Bay Bridge, and damaged my old neighborhood, the Marina District. Quite unexpectedly, Dave Burgin was again in the area, heading up the four publications of the Alameda Newspaper Group, and hired me as a columnist. What we thought would be a leisurely sojourn in the East Bay was, instead, a mad scramble.

Because of those events, I wasn't aware of the struggle between my former colleagues and Ed Moose over the union contract, which was up for renewal (or refusal) in mid-summer 1988. When I finally read Fimrite's book, I was surprised to learn I was the cause of much of the strife. He wrote:"[Arlene and Marcy] have felt an increasing sense of isolation since first Sofi and then Judy left. They also objected to Ed's apparent conclusion that the union beef was all Judy's doing. Judy was a vocal advocate of Local 2, they agree, but it was wrong to say it was all her fault, and yet, says Arlene, 'You heard it all the time'…"

Until then, I was unaware of my super power: Trouble-Making via Telekinesis.

Fimrite's account of The Square weaves together character profiles, bygone saloons of North Beach, references to writers and sports figures, the acquisition and development of WSB&G by Ed and Sam, the role of Mary Etta, and capably sketched in the delights of a place that had enraptured him. Two areas received the most focus: Les Lapins Sauvages, which he had chronicled from the beginning, and the unfolding union dispute and what that signified for the continued existence of WSB&G.

His descriptions of Ed's obnoxious behavior on the softball field, which could have imperiled their friendship, were masterfully handled, but he mostly hewed to the wonderfulness of it all. Yet again, Fimrite recounted the origins of the famous softball team, which began with the duping of Steve Spurrier, and the ongoing duping of other teams that thought they were gathered for a fun event rather than another notch on the Ed Moose Ego Belt. The growth of team's history and the addition of celebrity players were revisited. The names of team stalwarts were noted, and who doesn't like being recognized for being part of a once-upon-a-time phenomenon? The oft-told tales, with the addition of new away games, were again told.

In his book, Fimrite was carrying on, what had been, a mutually advantageous relationship. He was the correspondent-in-chief in a city that seemed to have an insatiable appetite for Ed Moose and Ed's softball saga. For his part, Ed could rely on favorable reportage and Fimrite's standing as a sports' writer to open publication doors. Early on, *Sport Illustrated* published a 17-page Fimrite article, complete with cartoon illustrations, about the San Francisco softball team (17 pages!) The affiliation was beneficial to both of them and they never seemed to tire of the fodder or the format.

The other focus of attention was the union dispute and the forth-coming contract deadline. Again, Fimrite's approach was even-handed. He noted how Ed's dark side complicated the union dispute. He sympathetically presented the conflicted feelings of my friends, who loved WSB&G, but felt principles for worker protection had to be defended. [Reportedly, Ed hated the book because "It was too nice to the staff."] I was proud to read how Marcy and Arlene headed up an employee committee that included waiters, Rick Snyder and Jim Gallup, to answer Ed's Doom's Day rhetoric. Paraphrased as follows:

Washington Square Bar & Grill was going to collapse like the House of Usher. Disappear into a black hole. Spontaneously combust. Cease to exist. And it was the fault of those wascally workers and their union. Thousands of WSB&G fans around the country were begging Ed to save the place. The employees were fouling their own nest, willfully destroying what he had built, depriving the City of its landmark watering hole. The situation was irreconcilable. The only solution was to sell WSB&G. The new owners would fire the ungrateful employees. Howls of execration. Rending of garments. Sack cloth and ashes to follow...

In those lines, I couldn't help but notice that Ed was just where he liked to be: The center of attention. Holding forth at full volume about his favorite topic, Ed Moose. Casting himself in the martyr role. Manipulating public opinion. Awash in hyperbole. ["It's like a Greek tragedy, I tell you.".…Ed Moose]

Ed's histrionics, as recorded by Fimrite, ran a gamut from personal fatigue ("After fifteen years, you're less romantic about it. You're tired. Just plain tired.") to the uncertainties of the future for a man, who was then sixty-ish ("In fact, I don't know what I'll do when the time comes. Maybe I'll go back to school or do something for Senator (Bill) Bradley.")

While Ron Fimrite was clearly striving for balanced reporting, there were areas that, I believe, he got wrong, one being the role that Mark Schachern purportedly played as manager.

Fimrite wrote: "When he first took charge, Mark saw only chaos. There was no real organization at all [said Mark]…The place was a lot of fun, but the food was mediocre and there were no controls over the staff. By ten o'clock at night, the bartenders were all shit-faced…For that matter, the whole staff was all screwed up. I was frankly agog…It was time to get down to business and make this thing work."

Put me down for some of that "frankly agog."

Mark's comments, which could have been lifted from a Mark Schachern Press Kit, managed to insult almost everyone. When he was hired as a waiter in 1979, the kitchen had been in the capable hands, for six years, of some of North Beach's most respected Italian chefs, Aldo Persich, Marcello Persi, and Silvio Conciatore. Mary Etta supervised. During the day, Ronnie Barber was an experienced cook and reliable mainstay. The food was never mediocre.

If the bartenders were drunk by ten o'clock, the solution should have been to send them home with a warning, get behind the bar himself, and fire them if they didn't change. I must have missed the time when Mark chastised the fearsome Tom Slater over the Green Chartreuse tradition. (Or did he join in?)

The remarks attributed to the teacher-turned-makeover-specialist disparaged the many fine bartenders (old stars and young up-and-comers) like Bobby McCambridge, Dennis O'Connor, Morty Miller, Bob Frugoli, Stuart Sharf and his brother Al, Bruce Crow, Gene Baskett, Michael McCourt, Seamus Coyle, and Cyril Boyce, all of whom passed through WSB&G.

As to the staff that was "all screwed up." The food servers were a remarkable self-adjusting group. If someone was abusive, disruptive, not a team player, or affecting the performance of the dining room by doing too much cocaine, that was made known and the misfits were pink-slipped. Besides the unfounded screwed-up-staff comment, Mark also called me out personally.

According to Fimrite, Mark claimed "[Judy's] serious involvement with the union and steadfast refusal to take the bosses seriously made her something of an irritant to Ed and Sam."

Now, my brain is a lint roller. It's full of happy memories, numerous regrets, and quite a few cringe-worthy recollections. I've sifted through the detritus of the lint roller and I find no basis for that statement. I remained friends with Maya Luckmann after she was hired by Local 2, but shop talk wasn't part of our socializing. In 1984, I joined the picket line for a union strike. (The order was all-hands on deck. Picketing is the payback for union benefits.)

I wasn't so much "seriously involved with the union" as I was seriously mistrustful of Ed, and warned my colleagues not to allow him to have more control over their lives. If the proposals were coming from Sam, I said, and Sam had still been conspicuously involved, that would be a different story. Most "Sam Hires" would have fire-walked for Sam, but our beloved boss had been pushed out of the picture.

In his place were Ed, and his minion, Mark, who Fimrite described as drinking CBAs as he jotted down their blame-shifting and character attacks. Nothing dissolves crocodile tears as effectively as a nice hot CBA. And, the Wharton School is rumored to offer a class in drinking and kvetching.

Apparently, Pat Lamborn, the Local 2 rep, was despised by Ed and Mark. My supposed "serious involvement" didn't include any significant interaction with Pat. And, I repeat, I was gone in September 1987, a full year before the contract dispute heated up.

As to not taking my bosses seriously. Utter foolishness. Of course, I was an irritant to Ed and I'd been seriously evading his unjust attempts to fire me for years. I don't believe Sam signed on to that statement at all. Sam was never shy about expressing irritation with anyone. He was never cross with me. Ever.

I was mystified that Fimrite accorded so much space and flattery to Mark. He wrote at length about Mark's managerial skills that supposedly transformed a barely functioning WSB&G, and reined in an undisciplined staff with a deft human touch, such that Mark sounded like the lovechild of Lee Iacocca and Mother Teresa.

The passages read like the longest, most lavish letter-of-recommendation ever written. Why did Fimrite pump up the Mark superlatives? Perhaps, he had pages to fill. Perhaps, he just liked the young man. Perhaps, something else.

As I've noted, the restaurant business can be complicated, but on some level, it can be deconstructed as Yogi Berra did with baseball complexity: *When they're hungry, we feed them. When we feed them, they pay us.* Finding a path between the complexity and simplicity is helpful for keeping one's head on straight.

The full title of Ron Fimrite's book was *The Square: The Story of a Saloon.* Fimrite was better prepared for the topic, by his many years as a faithful regular of WSB&G, than Mona Cochnar was, but he was still dependent on input from select people. He was, obviously, a veteran writer capable of filling in the details with research, interviews, embellished with a mature writing style. However, I feel the book is not a "story" as that term is generally understood: beginning, middle, and end.

Instead, the narrative closes with a cliffhanger. Ed had signed the union contract in August, 1988, but would he act upon his threat to sell WSB&G? ["Hell, I'm going to sell the fucking place"...Ed]

Here's how Fimrite described the groundwork laid for finding a buyer: "A high-powered downtown real-estate outfit had been employed to that end, and in furtherance of its quest for a buyer, the company produced a videotape extolling the joint's unique virtues."

Moreover, Ed had floated "a million dollars," as the amount it would take to buy WSB&G, which everyone knew would only buy the façade, not the animating spirit.

Ironically, Ed's quest to be the embodiment of WSB&G, had a backfired. Without him, the dollar-wise value of the saloon was reduced, if not to fire sale levels, at least to a bidding game for restaurant speculators. Why didn't Fimrite wait to write the story when it was complete? The omission of an ending is unsatisfying. Who bought the place and for how much? What happened to the partnership? What happened to the characters Fimrite chose to highlight? Why the cliffhanger?

As devotees of the legendary saloon know, WSB&G was sold. Ed announced the end of his ownership to the staff ten days before Christmas 1989. In effect, they were fired. As one bitter employee said, "Merry fucking Christmas!" By New Year's Eve 1989, the doors were locked.

In 1990, the new owner, Peter Lomax, took over. Lomax was an affable Englishman with an extensive hotelier and restaurant resume, who operated the well-regarded Monroe's Restaurant on

Lombard Street, which was also a union shop. He and Moose were longtime friends. Lomax did not reopen WSB&G as a union shop.

Predictably, some of the magic dissipated, as did the acclaimed staff members. Marcy went to work at Stars for celebrity chef, Jeremiah Tower. Arlene worked at several notable restaurants before starting her successful florist business, Violetta Flowers. Sofi became a yoga instructor with a devoted following. Bobby Ryder, and his son, Tyler, moved to Portland, Oregon, with the aim of getting out of the restaurant business. Rick Snyder went back to school to become a math teacher. Gary Epting continued to be a provocative painter.

The option to reapply for a job at the Lomax-owned WSB&G was precluded by two people, who were retained. Oddly, Ed Moose and Mark Schachern were kept on as some sort of transition team. They definitely were not going rehire any of the union supporters regardless of their popularity with customers.

While Lomax was a longtime friend of Ed's, he must have been a myopic pal indeed, if he thought Ed Moose could step aside as the Large Fromage and accept a subordinate role in the biscotti box he had transformed into a famous destination. With Moose onsite, what was Mark's function in the WSB&G reset? In addition, Lomax was trying to interest his two sons in the restaurant business and they were on the scene. If ever there was a case of too many cooks spoiling the broth, that was it. Inevitably, the broth was going to boil over.

Had Fimrite withheld publication until 1990, there might have been lots of juicy bits to include. I began to question why the story seemed to be truncated and prematurely published. Why was a narrative without a conclusive ending, something editors are usually pretty firm about, green lighted for publication?

The Square: The Story of a Saloon was published by Taylor Publishing Company. I learned that Taylor, self-described as a "Print Shop in Dallas, Texas," was one of the leading publishers of yearbooks in the United States. It was also a book bindery, capable of producing hard cover books in short to medium length runs. That sounded like, what in those days was called, a vanity press. How many books were in the run, how was it distributed, and who paid for them?

Not surprisingly, Taylor Publishing no longer has invoices from the 1980s and was unable to provide particulars. So, what could I glean from the book itself? The formatting of the book, typography, cover design, and book jacket were designed by Lurelle Cheverie, an artist and designer with many book designs. So, top tier talent.

I didn't understand the discrepancy between publication dates, 1988 in most cases and 1989 in a few. Amazon lists the publication date as January 1, 1988. How was that possible when the book references events taking place in July and August of 1988 and that Ed, in 1989, was planning a Moscow softball trip?

The title (or copyright) page of the Taylor published book has copyright 1988, but also notes "Library of Congress Cataloging-in-Publication Data" which is a bibliographic record sent to the L of C for a book that has not yet been published. Other announced publication dates (January 1, 1989 and April 1989) don't comport with the timeline of events in the book.

The title page also lists an introduction by Tom Wolfe. Instead, the intro was written by Dan Jenkins. Taken altogether, did those trifles add up to anything interesting? For decades, Ron Fimrite had been an obliging Boswell to Ed's softball biography. Was *The Square: The Story of a Saloon* another collaboration between the two?

When I mentioned to Marcy that I'd learned the book was self-published, she responded with one of her funny stories. "I've known that for years. I wanted to buy a second copy of Ron's book and asked him where it was available. He said there were hundreds of copies in his garage."

The temperature of the broth being tended by all those cooks and the fate of WS&G was laid out in a *Chronicle* article from

December 28, 1992, written by Sam Whiting and titled "The North Beach Bar War."

Whiting noted that WSB&G closed New Year's Eve 1989 and (precipitously) reopened two weeks later under new owner, Peter Lomax. Supposedly WSB&G sold for $500,000 which was shared by Ed and Sam. The sale included a non-competition clause that prohibited Ed Moose from opening another restaurant for two years.

Ed's sojourn as *auld lang syne* meeter-and-greeter at the saloon he once owned ended with rancor. He stomped out after one year, citing the inability to work with Lomax as his boss. Some would say that's richly ironic. Not me, of course.

Once again, he was at loose ends. Prior to selling his "fucking place," he considered his next moves ["Maybe I'll going back to school or do something with Senator Bradley."]

A year later, after exiting his former business, he was again pondering the future. The article noted his speculations: "Moose had big plans to stay away from restaurants and saloons. He would go back to school, study Greek, computers, go to work for Major League Baseball."

Good grief, all that reads like the ramblings of a pimply-faced sophomore in need of a high school guidance counselor.

In fact, the solution was obvious. Moose as food and booze purveyor was the only success on his resume, and the attention that came with it was oxygen. On Columbus Day (October 12, 1992) Ed opened Moose's Restaurant on Stockton Street across Washington Square Park from Lomax's WSB&G, shaving several months off the non-competition clause. Tacky and self-serving as that was, it wasn't the main bone of contention between the two owners.

The subtitle of Whiting's article was "It's not really about food or customers, it's about softball." Apparently, Lomax assumed the rights to the Penny Pitching contests and Les Lapins Sauvage softball games transferred with the purchase of Washington Square

Bar & Grill. Moose disagreed. Exactly when he disagreed was not addressed.

During the year Ed worked for Lomax, there must have been the annual Penny Pitching contest in February and the annual Mothers' Day softball game. Surely, those cornerstones of the calendar didn't go dormant. So, I imagine, Moose's *guardian ad litem* claim to the softballers wasn't exerted until he opened his new restaurant. Like the medieval Schism that resulted in two popes, the outcome was two softball teams competing for the loyalty of the faithful.

The split was so acrimonious, the two owners refused to enter each other's premises. Supposedly, Ed wouldn't even walk the short section of Powell Street in front of WSB&G. Chris Sullivan, the retired cop, who was a foundational member of the softball team and friend of both men, tried unsuccessfully to broker a truce between the adversaries. Instead, he shuttled between the two establishments, spending his discretionary income out of divided loyalty, as did many longtime WSB&G customers.

Whiting's 1992 article was in a friend's file and sent to me 30 years later. I was flabbergasted the softball saga, which seemed hackneyed at the end of the 1980s, had been renewed as a PR vehicle in the 1990s. But a PR vehicle for what? One man's team that incidentally was attached to a saloon? When Ed's priority was so invested in his traveling show, how much attention had he ever really paid to WSB&G? Was the saloon so many of us loved, just the farm team for his ego?

Ed's ridiculous fixation with the Wild Rabbits rattled what remained of my respect for his remarkable talents. And, undermined my perceptions of WSB&G. Was my personal Rashomon actually Kabuki?

Did others arrive at that feeling, too? Obituaries, which are written by families, recount the high points and favorite activities of the loved one who's passed. Christopher B. Sullivan's obituary, published in 2011 in the *Chronicle*, notes he raised money for St.

Anthony's Dining Room via the Penny Pitch contests, but makes no mention of his long-time participation in Ed's softball team.

To prepare for this memoir, I wanted to hear Mark Schachern's side of the story. For 30+ years, a quote from him in Fimrite's book has depicted me as a villainess, who initiated the demise of the beloved San Francisco saloon. Me? Whose every endeavor was shaded with the sense of Not Enough?

Not the monomaniacal Ed Moose pursuing the great white whale of public adulation with Ahab-like obsession? Not Mark, his compliant Queequeg, ready to harpoon the staff, from which he had arisen, to help accomplish the Ahab mission? (Melville metaphor exaggerated for comic effect.)

The record was long overdue for correction. And, Time has a way of burying hatchets. Even the small grievances I assigned to Mark are long in the past. Thus, I started trying to contact him to talk as two people, who shared a great experience from different vantage points.

When we finally spoke in March 2022, Mark was congenial and seemingly comfortable filling in missing details. We laughingly recalled characters events and Ed's PR genius, Helmut's antics, and (groan!) the softball team. When I asked how the sale of WSB&G affected him, I was astonished at what Mark revealed.

For starters, I learned only then, that Lomax had retained Mark as part of the new operation. Mark was hoping to "take over" management (he did have a fulsome letter of recommendation on file) and parlay the 10% partnership he purchased with a loan from Sam into buying the saloon himself sometime in the future. However, he couldn't get along with the two Lomax sons, who he called "idiots" and quit after six months.

Quarrels with the staff, without Pat Lamborn to blame? Some might call that Karma. Not me. Karma supposedly corrects misdeeds. From what I've seen, miscreants thrive and Karma works even less than the Maytag Repairman. But it is funny.

I queried Mark about a theory I had, that Ed was playing a long game, that even in 1988 when the contract loomed, he was planning to shed the ramshackle premises for a larger, sleeker location, divest himself of obsolete partnerships, and open a non-union business. Mark denied that, and offered an astonishing alternative.

Ed and Lomax had a scheme for a sham sale. Lomax would buy WSB&G, they would bust the union, then Ed would repurchase Washington Square Bar & Grill. (Maybe Ed should have gone back to school—law school—where he'd encounter something called *fraudulent transfer*.) And what about that high-powered downtown real-estate outfit and the video seeking a buyer described by Fimrite? Misdirection—or fiction?

However improbable the scheme sounds; it makes crazy sense. Had WSB&G reverted to Ed after a couple years, eyebrows would have raised, certainly at Local 2. But Ed probably believed in his ability to schmooze his way out of any shady situation, just as he explained shorting the non-competition agreement to open Moose's Restaurant.

Ed told Mark that he was walking across Washington Square Park when someone said "Didn't you used to be Ed Moose?"

That little dig (or poorly phrased question) supposedly propelled Ed to borrow two million dollars to buy the building that formerly housed the Figone furniture store and another million to renovate the space. Isn't the outlay of other people's money the standard response to snark? Ed claimed he arm-twisted Sam, who was retired and resistant to further involvement in the bar business, into investing in Moose's. Mark said Ed also tapped his wealthy friend and steadfast softballer, Herb Allen.

So, Ed's self-esteem was supposed to be paramount. He needed a place to be enthroned. If he could have bided his time, restrained his temper, and let the sham sale play out, that throne could once again have been Washington Square Bar & Grill. Instead, he fell out with Lomax and had to create Moose's Restaurant as a big eff you to the Englishman. Or, so it seems to me. Again, can the dead offer any clarification?

Godfrey "Peter" Lomax's obituary, published in 2016, says Lomax had retired from the restaurant business but "[The] restaurant business was in his blood and he soon went to help out his friend, Ed Moose, who owned the Washington Square Bar & Grill…Ed retired shortly thereafter and Peter became the proprietor for the next 5 years until he retired."

Reading between those lines, seems to further confirm Mark's claim of a sham sale. And reinforces the observation that "No good deed goes unpunished." However, the WS&G staff can be absolved of any residual guilt that the union dispute killed the legendary saloon. At the time, when Ed could have reclaimed WSB&G, union free, he chose a temper tantrum.

After a five-year tenure under Peter Lomax, Washington Square Bar & Grill was purchased by Peter Osborne, an experienced restauranteur, who rejuvenated the failing saloon for a time. Dick Fregulia said "Peter [Osborne] was like a young Moose. He was a bear-hug kind of guy with personality…he had a presence people liked."

Respecting WSB&G's history and unique place in the City, Osborne announced there'd be a celebration of the saloon's 25th anniversary. Word of the 1998 get together reached me in Ohio, where Mike and I owned a small horse farm. When we left the Bay

Area, I assumed San Francisco was just a plane ride away and that I could return often. I under-estimated the demands of horse and farm ownership. Horses are catastrophe magnets. Farms, whether new or ramshackle, as ours was, constantly fall apart.

The 25th anniversary would be my first trip back to the City that held so much magic and memories. I arranged for horse sitters, booked a room at the Arlene's Misspent Youth Hostel, and notified Maya to meet me on Powell Street.

We entered the front door to find the premises wonderfully unchanged. Thankfully, no one fixed what wasn't broken. The black-framed photos on the burnt sienna walls were still there. The tables draped in white linen were still inviting. The brass rail at the service bar where we queued up to fill our cocktail orders still gave off a metallic glow. However, the anniversary didn't have the pizazz of an Ed Moose event. Instead, it felt like someone put out a six pack of Bud Light and a bowl of pretzels, and called it a party. But, the chance to see old friends was the point.

Maya and I hadn't been there long when Specs Simmons arrived and the three of us got a table and ordered drinks. Manuel Sauceda, who was the heart and workhorse of the kitchen, was still there. He stepped away from his duties to say hello and wrap his big boxer arms around me.

Then, we resumed our chat with Specs. In my view, Specs was the counter point to Ed Moose. His business, 12 Adler Place, had its own fervent following and Specs was a much-loved figure in North Beach. But, none of that ever went to his head. He didn't get caught in a relentless quest of self-aggrandizement. His saloon has been named a "legacy" landmark and continues to this day under his daughter Elly and granddaughter Maralisa.

While we swapped stories, someone came to the table and said "Sam is outside. But says he won't come in because he doesn't want Judy and Maya to fuss over him."

For a moment, my mind lingered on "Sam is *outside.*" My hope in attending the reunion was to see him wearing a jaunty red neckerchief and waving me toward the bar in a replay of our first meeting. Why was he outside? Was he, unbeknownst to me, observing Ed's boycott of the landmark they created?

Instead, I focused on Sam supposedly avoiding Maya and I making a fuss over him. How typical of Sam to reject what he most wanted, to stiff arm his emotions, to say No because the answer might be Yes. Maya and I both understood that.

She got up immediately and went outside. I felt it would be rude to abruptly end my conversation with one dear friend for another, and thought "What harm can come from chatting with Specs for a few more minutes, then going out to greet Sam?"

When I went outside, he was nowhere to be seen. I looked in both directions for sight of him. I wish I'd chased along the sidewalks in search of him. Or hailed a cab and told the driver, "We have to find a quirky, little man who's somewhere in this neighborhood."

Or somehow caught up Sam in a warm embrace to say: Thank you for all the wit and laughter we shared. Thank you for the wonderful experience you made possible. Thank you for allowing me to be among the stars of the bar.

But he was gone. And, nothing can mitigate my regret for those delayed minutes that weren't meant to be harmful, but cost me a moment that can't be recalled. I never had a chance to see him again. Sam died in 2002. Of all the things in Life that are Not Enough, the foremost is Time.

Epilogue

I n 2012, Ed Moose died at the age of 81. He broke an ankle in a fall and several surgical attempts at repair resulted in a fatal staph infection. He successfully operated Moose's from 1990 to 2005, another long run that defied the mortality rate for restaurants in a City where businesses of all kinds were under duress. For 32 years, he was the reigning impresario of the City's restauranteurs, first with Washington Square Bar & Grill, then Moose's Restaurant. He masterfully manipulated the media's seemingly endless appetite for his colorful personality to keep his name before the public.

So great was the devotion of WSB&G's clientele to the famous saloon Ed created that they continued to patronize the remnant he left behind as it changed hands several times. When every resuscitation failed, the faithful collected the relics and memorabilia and persuaded the San Francisco Public Library to establish a shrine to the legendary saloon.

Tom Brokaw, former NBC news anchor, sometime softballer, and friend, eulogized Ed, saying "He led the life he always wanted. It was a life filled with saloons, cronies, chilled martinis, politics, baseball, jazz, and laughs built around a great meal. He was the last of a breed."

Many of us partook of that life and have no regrets. But, there came a time when a rebellious liver, or lethal hangover, or ennui with clever bon mots, or surfeit of shallow conversations, signaled the need for change. The time, as Sofi said, when one accepts that life will never again be as much fun.

"Were we alumni of WSB&G?" I asked Marcy, "Or survivors?"

The question, I daresay, is uncomfortable for those of us, who were employed during WSB&G's heyday—and, saw the saloon life consume our beloved and brilliant comrade, Neil Riofski. He died in 2003 at the age of 55. As his drinking became progressively worse, his bartender resume descended from WSB&G to Moose's where he was employed with the proviso that he couldn't drink, then to Capp's Corner, and finally dive bars in the Tenderloin. The love and concern of his legion of friends could not deter the terrible trajectory.

At the end, Neil was staying with a friend, who was also battling alcoholism. The two of them resolved to go on one last bender before entering rehab. The following morning, the friend discovered Neil had died in the early morning hours.

The day I met Sam Dietsch, he was looking for "…[A] star, a star of the bar." For me, Neil, with his beautiful soul and gloriously gifted mind, was the brightest star that ever passed through Washington Square Bar & Grill.

Made in United States
Orlando, FL
07 September 2024

51256214R00126